200 easy vegetarian dishes

hamlyn | all colour cookbook

200 easy vegetarian dishes

Denise Smart

An Hachette UK Company
www.hachette.co.uk

First published in Great Britain in 2014 by Hamlyn
a division of Octopus Publishing Group Ltd
Endeavour House, 189 Shaftesbury Avenue
London WC2H 8JY
www.octopusbooks.co.uk

ISBN: 978-0-600-62820-0

A CIP catalogue record for this book is available from the
British Library

Printed and bound in China

1 2 3 4 5 6 7 8 9 10

Both metric and imperial measurements have
been given in all recipes. Use one set of measurements
only, and not a mixture of both.

Standard level spoon measurements are used in all recipes
1 tablespoon = 15 ml spoon
1 teaspoon = 5 ml spoon

Ovens should be preheated to the specified temperature –
if using a fan-assisted oven, follow the manufacturer's
instructions for adjusting the time and temperature.

Fresh herbs should be used unless otherwise stated.
Medium eggs should be used unless otherwise stated.
Freshly ground black pepper should be used unless
otherwise stated.

This book includes dishes made with nuts and nut
derivatives. It is advisable for people with known allergic
reactions to nuts and nut derivatives or those who may be
potentially vulnerable to these allergies, such as pregnant
and nursing mothers, invalids, the elderly, babies and
children, to avoid dishes made with these. It is prudent to
check the labels of all pre-prepared ingredients for the
possible inclusion of nut derivatives.

contents

introduction

introduction

First, let's start by clarifying what a vegetarian diet is. The Vegetarian Society defines a vegetarian as: 'Someone who lives on a diet of grains, pulses, nuts, seeds, vegetables and fruits, with or without the use of dairy products and eggs. A vegetarian does not eat any meat, poultry, game, fish, shellfish or by-products of slaughter.' People may choose to follow a vegetarian diet for various reasons, including religious, social, lifestyle, moral, environmental and health.

Today, being a vegetarian, cooking for a vegetarian in your family or choosing to have a couple of meat-free days a week is so much easier, with supermarkets and health food shops offering a range of ingredients for making tasty and satisfying vegetarian dishes. Many people perceive vegetarian cooking as being time-consuming and featuring heavy stews of beans and lentils, nut loaves and omelettes. This book aims to dispel that myth. It provides 200 recipes to help you create simple, flavourful vegetarian feasts, with inspirational ideas for easy, nutritious dishes for breakfast and brunch, starters and snacks, main meals, soups and stews, salads and sides, breads and baking and desserts. So there's sure to be something here to please all tastes, vegetarian and non-vegetarian alike.

ingredients

For vegetarians, avoiding certain products can be tricky. For example, animal fat and ingredients such as gelatine may be used in manufactured foods. Rennet, which is extracted from the stomach lining of cows, is often used in cheese making. Also, some jars of curry pastes may contain shrimp. In many cases, there are vegetarian alternatives to these ingredients, so it is advisable to take time to check out food labels.

The following is a brief guide to the ingredients commonly used in the recipes.

pulses and beans

Gone are the days when you have to soak dried beans and pulses overnight. Cans of beans can make a nutritious speedy meal, just drain, rinse under cold water and drain again well before using. It is worth keeping a good supply of the following in your store cupboard.

Red kidney beans These red beans make a popular choice for soups, stews, casseroles and hot spicy dishes, such as Quick Vegetable Mole on page 146.

Black beans This member of the kidney bean family can be used in stews, soups and salads or as a substitute for red kidney beans.

Butter beans These large, flattish, creamy white beans have a mild flavour and floury texture, and absorb lots of flavour. They are great cooked in stews or soups – for a quick lunch, try the Butter Bean & Vegetable Soup on page 142.

Cannellini beans These small, creamy white members of the kidney bean family are ideal for salads, such as the Cannellini & Green Bean Salad on page 158.

Dried red split lentils These lentils need no soaking and quickly cook down to a purée. They are commonly used in Indian-style dishes, like the Spinach & Tomato Dhal on page 152.

Green and Puy lentils Smaller than green lentils, Puy lentils have a great texture and a mild peppery taste. Buy them in cans or precooked in packs.

Chickpeas These look like small hazelnuts and have a nutty flavour. Featuring in Middle Eastern, Mediterranean and Indian cooking, they are added to curries and stews or used in salads or dips such as hummus. Try roasting them with spices such as in Moroccan Spiced Chickpeas on page 44.

Soya beans These can be bought podded and frozen, requiring just a few minutes' cooking. Delicious in salads, soups or noodle dishes.

Couscous Originating from North Africa, couscous is the staple ingredient in the North African diet. These tiny granules are made from steamed and dried semolina formed into tiny pellets. Couscous is a popular alternative to rice and pasta, and has a light, fluffy texture that is a little bland in flavour but which readily soaks up the flavours of other ingredients. Serve it with the Chickpea & Aubergine Tagine on page 150, or for a change, try giant or wholewheat couscous.

Rice While many people in the West think of rice as a simple side dish, rice is exciting when cooked as a meal in its own right and easily absorbs other flavours. The different cultivation techniques, as well as crossbreeding of rice, have resulted in thousands of varieties, including sticky rices, wild rices and fragrant rices. Keep a selection of brown, jasmine, basmati, risotto and pudding rice. Grown on hillsides, in soil or in irrigated waters, either deep or shallow.

grains and rice
Here are some grains worth keeping on hand in your store cupboard – use wholegrains where possible.

Quinoa This is actually a seed, from South America, which has become very popular over the past few years. It is high in protein, quick to cook and has a chewy, slightly nutty flavour. There are also red and black varieties. Quinoa is perfect for soaking up sauces, or why not start the day with a bowl of the Quinoa Porridge with Raspberries on page 36.

Bulgar wheat This wholewheat grain is steam-dried and cracked, needing only a brief soaking before serving. It's popular in Middle Eastern cooking, the best-known example being the salad dish tabbouleh.

pasta and noodles
Pasta is made from durum flour and eggs, and is available fresh and dried and in many shapes, such as penne, farfalle, fusilli, tagliatelle, spaghetti and linguine, to name just a few. Stuffed pasta, such as ravioli and tortellini, are sold chilled in supermarkets filled with delicious vegetarian fillings such as spinach and ricotta or pumpkin and goats' cheese. Pasta makes a great accompaniment

or a main meal. Gnocchi is a small potato dumpling for tossing in sauce or butter.

Noodles can be made from rice, wheat or buckwheat and are available fresh or dried. You can buy a huge selection of noodles in your supermarket or from Asian food shops. Varieties include soba, udon, somen, bean thread, ramen, vermicelli or flat rice noodles. Use them in soups, pad Thai and stir-fries, or as an accompaniment to a main dish.

food to keep in the fridge

Stock up on the following ingredients regularly, and you will be ready to cook up a whole range of tempting vegetarian dishes.

tofu

Also called bean curd, tofu is made from soya beans. It's extremely versatile and can be used in stir-fries, casseroles and soups. Although it's quite bland in taste, with the addition of flavourings and marinades it can be delicious. Try the Tandoori Tofu Bites on page 58.

cheese

Cheese is a good source of protein for vegetarians, but always check the label to ensure that it is suitable for vegetarians and doesn't contain animal rennet. Some hard cheeses are still made with animal rennet, although increasingly cheese is being made with 'microbial enzymes', widely used in the industry because they are a consistent and inexpensive coagulant.

The term 'microbial enzyme' means that it is a synthetically developed coagulant, while the term 'vegetable rennet' indicates one derived from a vegetable source. Soft cheeses such as cream cheese and cottage cheese are manufactured without rennet. Some cottage cheeses, however, may contain gelatine, which is derived from animal sources.

The following are cheeses suitable for vegetarians and useful to keep in the fridge:

Goats' cheese Made from goats' milk, this cheese has a tangy flavour and can be either soft and creamy or it is bought hard, so is suitable for grating.

Feta This creamy, crumbly white Greek cheese is traditionally made from ewes' milk or a mixture of ewes' and goats' milk but is now sometimes made using cows' milk. It has a salty flavour and is perfect in salads, with couscous or pasta.

Mozzarella An Italian fresh or unripened cheese traditionally made from water buffaloes' milk around the Naples area. A firm but creamy cheese it tastes like fresh milk with a slightly sour edge. It melts well and has a unique stretchiness, making it the classic pizza-topping cheese. Used in Margherita Scone-based Pizza, page 186.

Cheddar Made from cows' milk, a lot of Cheddar is now produced using vegetarian rennet. Mature Cheddar has great flavour.

Vegetarian pasta cheese This is a great vegetarian alternative to Parmesan cheese, for use in risottos or pasta dishes.

Taleggio From Northern Italy, this mildly flavoured whole cows' milk cheese has a soft texture and a fruity, creamy character. It is used in Macaroni Cheese with Spinach on page 98.

Ricotta This soft Italian curd cheese is made from whey, which is drained and then lightly 'cooked'. It is creamy with a slightly grainy texture and delicate flavour. Relatively low in fat it is used in many Italian dishes.

other useful fridge ingredients

Eggs Keep a mixture of medium and large eggs. Always buy free-range, preferably organic, when available.

Vegetables Keep a good selection of green leafy vegetables, peppers, onions, tomatoes, carrots, sweet potatoes, parsnips, squashes, potatoes and mushrooms.

Ready-rolled puff pastry Fresh or frozen.

Fresh pasta, noodles and gnocchi

Milk, yogurt, butter, cream and crème fraîche.

flavourings & sauces

A simple way of adding exciting flavours to meals is using a selection of herbs and spices (fresh or dried), pastes or bottled sauces and condiments. Have the following to hand:

Harissa paste A fiery North African paste that is orangey-red in colour. A mixture of peppers, dried red chillies, garlic, caraway seeds, ground cumin and coriander, tomato purée, salt and olive oil. Used as a condiment or as an ingredient, it provides a real flavour boost.

Moroccan and Middle Eastern spice mixes Such as baharat, zahtar and ras-el-hanout.

Curry pastes Such as tikka and korma. Be careful when choosing Thai-style pastes, as many of these may contain shrimp.

Dark and light soy sauce Great for adding saltiness to a dish instead of Thai fish sauce.

Chipotle paste A smoky chilli paste used in Mexican dishes.

Nuts and seeds Pine nuts, cashew nuts, walnuts and peanuts. Sunflower seeds, pumpkin seeds and linseed.

Oils Sunflower, groundnut, olive and sesame oils.

Vegetable stock Use good-quality stock cubes or bouillon powder, or fresh vegetable stock.

Spices A selection, including ground coriander, ground cumin, cumin seeds, paprika, smoked paprika, curry powder, chilli powder, turmeric and mustard seeds.

Dried herbs Dried mixed herbs and oregano.

Fresh herbs Such as coriander, basil, parsley, chives, thyme, rosemary and tarragon. Grow in pots on your window ledge or garden.

Mustard Wholegrain, Dijon and English.

Tomato ketchup, wasabi paste, sweet chilli sauce

Chopped and plum tomatoes, coconut milk

Lemon grass, kaffir lime leaves and curry leaves.

ensuring a balanced diet

A vegetarian diet can supply all the nutrients needed for health and vitality, and eating vegetarian can make it easier to achieve the desired '5 a day' consumption of fresh fruit and vegetables. It can be useful to eat food from the following five food 'groups'.

protein

This can come from many sources, the main ones are as follows. Pulses (peas, beans and lentils), are an excellent and inexpensive source of protein and also contain minerals such as iron, zinc and calcium. Soya products, which include tofu and Quorn™, contain a form of 'myco-protein' and these are available as mince, burgers, fillets and sausages. The third source are eggs, dairy products, nuts and seeds. These contain zinc, valuable calcium and iron, as well as protein.

fruit and vegetables

Aim to eat at least five portions a day, where one portion weighs about 80 g (3 oz). Try to choose a wide variety of different-coloured fruit and vegetables, which will provide a balanced mix of nutrients.

carbohydrate-rich foods

Potatoes, pasta, rice and pulses provide sustained energy from carbohydrates, as well as B vitamins and fibre. One-third of your food intake should be made up of carbohydrate so try to eat one food from this group each meal.

dairy products or alternatives

These are needed for protein and calcium. At least three portions should be eaten each day, where one portion is a 200 ml (7 fl oz) glass of milk, a 150 ml (¼ pint) pot of yogurt or a 30 g (1 oz) piece of cheese. Alternatives include rice milk, dried figs, nuts, green vegetables and soya products, such as tofu.

vitamins and minerals

Iron is vital for the maintenance of healthy red blood cells and to prevent anaemia. Vegetarian sources include eggs, leafy green vegetables, wholemeal bread, molasses, dried fruit (especially apricots), pulses, fortified breakfast cereals, peanut butter and pumpkin, sesame and sunflower seeds. Iron from vegetable sources is not as easily absorbed as that from animal sources. If eaten with food rich in vitamin C, the body's absorption of iron

is enhanced. Drink fruit juice with breakfast cereal, or squeeze fresh lemon juice on green vegetables and salads.

kitchen equipment

So you have the ingredients to hand and it's time to cook. All you need are a few items of kitchen equipment.

tools for the job

Pans The first and most important tool is a large, heavy-based frying pan or wok. Make sure the frying pan has a flameproof handle so that it can go from the hob to under the grill. You will also need a selection of different-sized good-quality saucepans with lids, as well as at least two good-sized baking sheets. A griddle pan is a good idea, too.

Knives Make sure you have at least two good-quality knives, a small one for paring and slicing and a larger one for chopping. Also keep a few chopping boards.

Food processor Invest in a good-quality food processor and whizzing up pastes and pestos, blending soups and chopping fruits and nuts will suddenly seem as easy as pie.

Bowls Ensure you have a selection of sizes.

Colander and sieve You will need a good-sized colander and a fine-meshed sieve to make cooking family meals easier.

Grater One that you can hold comfortably, has many slicing options and, most importantly, is sharp, will feel like a help rather than a hindrance, and microplanes are fantastic for quickly removing the rind from citrus fruits.

Measuring tools A set of kitchen scales and measuring spoons, along with a measuring jug, are essential for measuring ingredients.

Other basic tools These include stirring spoons, slotted spoons, a vegetable peeler, balloon whisk and tongs.

get cooking!

With a stocked store cupboard and fridge, the correct equipment and 200 recipes to choose from, you are now ready to go.

breakfast & brunch

honey-roasted granola

Serves **4**
Preparation time **10 minutes**,
  plus cooling
Cooking time **25–30 minutes**

5 tablespoons **clear honey**
2 tablespoons **sunflower oil**
250 g (8 oz) **porridge oats**
50 g (2 oz) **hazelnuts**,
  roughly chopped
50 g (2 oz) **blanched
  almonds**, roughly chopped
50 g (2 oz) **dried cranberries**
50 g (2 oz) **dried blueberries**

Heat the honey and oil together gently in a
small saucepan.

Mix the oats and nuts together thoroughly in a large
bowl. Pour over the warm honey mixture and stir well
to combine.

Spread the mixture over a large nonstick baking sheet
and bake in a preheated oven, 150°C (300°F), Gas
Mark 2, for 20–25 minutes, stirring once, until golden.

Leave the granola to cool, then stir in the dried berries.
Serve with skimmed milk or low-fat bio yogurt and
fresh fruit. Any remaining granola can be stored in
an airtight container.

**For oven-baked chocolate, almond & cherry
granola**, mix the warmed honey and sunflower oil as
above with 2 tablespoons sifted cocoa powder. Mix
the porridge oats and 100 g (3½ oz) blanched almonds
together in a large bowl. Pour over the warm honey
mixture and stir well to combine. Bake as above and
leave to cool, then stir in 100 g (3½ oz) dried cherries.
Serve with milk. ·

tomato, pepper & egg tortillas

Serves **4**
Preparation time **15 minutes**
Cooking time **25–30 minutes**

1 tablespoon **olive oil**
1 small **onion**, finely chopped
1 **garlic clove**, crushed
1 **mild green chilli**, deseeded and finely chopped
1 small **green pepper**, cored, deseeded and thinly sliced
1 small **red pepper**, cored, deseeded and thinly sliced
400 g (13 oz) can **chopped tomatoes**
2 tablespoons **tomato ketchup**
4 **eggs**
4 **corn tortillas**
smoked paprika, for sprinkling
salt and **black pepper**

Heat the oil in a large frying pan with a lid, add the onion, garlic, chilli and peppers and cook over a medium heat, stirring frequently, for about 10–15 minutes until the peppers are soft. Stir in the tomatoes and ketchup and season with salt and pepper. Bring to the boil, then simmer for 5 minutes until thickened.

Make 4 shallow hollows in the tomato mixture with the back of a spoon and break an egg into each hollow. Cover the pan and cook over a low heat for about 5 minutes until just set.

Meanwhile, warm the tortillas according to the packet instructions. Place a tortilla on each warmed serving plate and carefully transfer the egg and tomato mixture on to each tortilla. Serve immediately, sprinkled with a little smoked paprika.

For breakfast mushroom quesadillas, heat 2 tablespoons olive oil in a large frying pan, add 1 small chopped onion, 1 crushed garlic clove and 1 finely chopped green chilli and cook gently for 2–3 minutes. Increase the heat, add 500 g (1 lb) mixed mushrooms, trimmed and roughly chopped, and cook for 4–5 minutes until they start to release their juice. Stir in 1 teaspoon lime juice and 2 tablespoons chopped parsley and cook for a further 5 minutes until the mushrooms are tender. Meanwhile, heat a large heavy-based frying pan over a medium heat, add 4 corn tortillas and heat for 30 seconds on each side until soft. Place a quarter of the mushroom mixture on one half of a tortilla, fold over and press down. Turn over and cook until the tortilla is slightly crispy. Repeat with the remaining tortillas and mushroom mixture.

sunshine breakfast muffins

Makes **10**
Preparation time **10 minutes**
Cooking time **20–25 minutes**

250 g (8 oz) **plain flour**
1 tablespoon **baking powder**
100 g (3½ oz) **porridge oats**
125 g (4 oz) **ready-to-eat
dried apricots**, chopped
50 g (2 oz) **dried cranberries**
2 tablespoons **mixed seeds,**
such as sunflower, linseed,
pumpkin and hemp
50 g (2 oz) **soft light
brown sugar**
½ teaspoon **salt**
2 **eggs**, lightly beaten
175 ml (6 fl oz) **milk**
75 ml (3 fl oz) **sunflower oil**
4 tablespoons **clear honey**

Line a 12-hole muffin tin with 10 paper muffin cases.

Sift the flour and baking powder together into a large bowl. Stir in the oats, dried fruits, seeds, sugar and salt with a metal spoon.

Beat the eggs, milk, oil and honey together in a jug. Pour over the dry ingredients and stir until only just combined – the batter should be lumpy and fairly runny.

Spoon the mixture into the muffin cases so that they are two-thirds full and bake on the top shelf of a preheated oven, 190°C (375°F), Gas Mark 5, for 20–25 minutes until risen and golden.

Leave to cool in the tin for 5 minutes, then transfer to a wire rack to cool completely.

For banana breakfast muffins, follow the above recipe to make the muffin mixture, using 125 g (4 oz) jumbo porridge oats in place of the oats and 50 g (2 oz) sultanas in place of the dried apricots and cranberries.

ricotta & blueberry pancakes

Serves **4**
Preparation time **10 minutes**
Cooking time **10–15 minutes**

250 g (8 oz) **ricotta cheese**
125 ml (4 fl oz) **milk**
3 **large eggs**, separated
100 g (3½ oz) **plain flour**
3 tablespoons **caster sugar**
1 teaspoon **baking powder**
finely grated rind of 1 **lemon**
125 g (4 oz) **fresh
   blueberries**
unsalted butter, for frying
lemon juice or **maple syrup**,
   to serve

Beat the ricotta with the milk and egg yolks in a large bowl. Stir in the flour, sugar, baking powder, lemon rind and blueberries until well combined.

Whisk the egg whites with a hand-held electric whisk in a separate large, grease-free bowl until they form soft peaks, then gently fold into the ricotta mixture with a large metal spoon.

Heat a little butter in a heavy-based frying pan over a medium heat. Add about one-quarter of the batter to the pan to make 3–4 pancakes about 7 cm (3 inches) in diameter and cook for 1–2 minutes on each side until golden and cooked through. Transfer the pancakes to a baking sheet and keep warm in a low oven while you repeat with the remaining batter, adding a little more butter to the pan as necessary.

Serve 3–4 pancakes per person, with lemon juice or maple syrup.

For Scotch pancakes with blueberry compote, place 200 g (7 oz) blueberries in a saucepan with 2 tablespoons caster sugar and 1 tablespoon lemon juice. Heat gently, stirring occasionally, until the blueberries start to burst and release their juice. Simmer for 2–3 minutes until jammy. Meanwhile, heat a griddle pan until hot, add 8 ready-made Scotch pancakes and cook for 1 minute on each side until heated through. Serve hot with the warm compote.

goats' cheese omelettes

Serves **4**
Preparation time **10 minutes**
Cooking time **20 minutes**

4 tablespoons **olive oil**
500 g (1 lb) mixed **red
  and yellow cherry
  tomatoes**, halved
a little **basil**, chopped, plus a
  few sprigs, to garnish
12 **eggs**
2 tablespoons **wholegrain
  mustard**
50 g (2 oz) **butter**
100 g (3½ oz) **soft goats'
  cheese**, diced
salt and **black pepper**
watercress, to garnish

Heat the oil in a frying pan, add the tomatoes and cook over a medium heat for 2–3 minutes until softened (you may have to do this in 2 batches). Add the basil and season to taste with salt and pepper, then transfer to a bowl and keep warm.

Beat the eggs with the mustard in a large bowl and season with salt and pepper.

Melt one-quarter of the butter in an omelette pan or small frying pan over a medium heat until it stops foaming, then swirl in one-quarter of the egg mixture. Fork over the omelette so that it cooks evenly. As soon as it is set on the bottom (but still a little runny in the middle), dot over a quarter of the goats' cheese and cook for a further 30 seconds. Carefully slide the omelette on to a warmed plate, folding it in half as you do so. Keep warm.

Repeat with the remaining mixture to make 3 more omelettes. Serve with the tomatoes, garnished with watercress and basil sprigs.

oven-baked sausage brunch

Serves **2**

Preparation time **10 minutes**

Cooking time **30 minutes**

1 tablespoon **sunflower oil**

4 **vegetarian sausages**

2 **potatoes**, scrubbed and cut into 1 cm (½ inch) cubes

4 mini **portobello mushrooms**, trimmed

2 **tomatoes**, halved

2 **large eggs**

black pepper

Heat the oil in a nonstick ovenproof dish or roasting dish in a preheated oven, 200°C (400°F), Gas Mark 6, until hot.

Add the sausages and potatoes to the hot oil and turn to coat in the oil. Cook in the oven for 10 minutes.

Remove the dish from the oven, add the mushrooms and tomatoes and turn with the sausages and potatoes to coat in the oil. Return to the oven and cook for a further 10–12 minutes until the potatoes are golden and the sausages are cooked through.

Make 2 separate spaces in the baked mixture and break an egg into each. Return to the oven and cook for a further 3–4 minutes until the eggs are softly set. Grind over some black pepper and serve immediately.

For sausage & tomato tortilla, cook 2 vegetarian sausages under a preheated medium grill for about 10 minutes, turning occasionally, until cooked through. Leave to cool slightly, then slice thickly. Meanwhile, boil 200 g (7 oz) thickly sliced new potatoes in a saucepan of boiling water for 6–8 minutes until tender, then drain well. Heat 1 tablespoon sunflower oil in a small frying pan with a flameproof handle, add the sausages and potatoes and cook for 2–3 minutes. Stir in 4 halved cherry tomatoes. Beat 3 eggs together, season well with salt and pepper and pour over the sausage mixture. Cook over a low heat for 8–10 minutes until just set. Sprinkle over 25 g (1 oz) grated Cheddar cheese, place the pan under a preheated high grill and cook for 2–3 minutes until the tortilla is golden brown on top and set. Serve cut into wedges.

mixed berry smoothie

Serves **2**

Preparation time **5 minutes**

1 small ripe **banana**,
  roughly chopped
175 g (6 oz) **fresh mixed
  berries**, such as raspberries,
  blueberries and strawberries
250 ml (8 fl oz) **low-fat** or
  fat-free vanilla bio yogurt
about 150 ml (¼ pint) **semi-
  skimmed milk**

Place the banana in a blender with the berries, yogurt and milk and blend until thick and smooth, adding a little more milk if you prefer a thinner consistency.

Divide the smoothie between 2 glasses and serve immediately.

For banana, oat & honey smoothie, place 1 roughly chopped ripe banana in a blender with 1 tablespoon each of clear honey and porridge oats. Add 300 ml (½ pint) semi-skimmed milk and blend until smooth. Divide the smoothie between 2 glasses and serve.

potato farls with mushrooms

Serves **2**
Preparation time **15 minutes**
Cooking time **12 minutes**

1 tablespoon **olive oil**
25 g (1 oz) **unsalted butter**
2 **shallots,** finely chopped
250 g (8 oz) **mixed
    mushrooms,** such as
    chestnut, portobello and
    button, trimmed and sliced
2 **garlic cloves,** chopped
1 tablespoon **lemon juice**
2 tablespoons chopped **flat
    leaf parsley**
2 **large eggs**
4 ready-made **potato farls,**
    toasted
salt and **black pepper**
1 tablespoon chopped **chives,**
    to garnish

Heat the oil with the butter in a frying pan over a high heat. Reduce the heat slightly, add the shallots and mushrooms and fry for 6 minutes, stirring occasionally, until the mushrooms are golden. Stir in the garlic and cook, stirring, for 1 minute.

Add the lemon juice to the mushroom mixture and season with salt and pepper.

Remove the pan from the heat and stir in the parsley. Keep warm while you poach the eggs.

Half-fill a separate frying pan with water and bring to a simmer. Break in the eggs and cook for 3 minutes.

Place 2 potato farls on each warmed serving plate and top with the mushroom mixture, then the eggs. Sprinkle with the chives and serve immediately.

For potato rösti with baked eggs & tomatoes, place 8 ready-made small frozen potato rösti in a roasting tin with 12 cherry tomatoes and drizzle with 1 tablespoon olive oil. Cook in a preheated oven, 200°C (400°F), Gas Mark 6, for 10 minutes. Remove from the oven and turn the röstis over. Return to the oven and cook for a further 6 minutes until golden. Break 2 eggs into the roasting tin and return to the oven for 2–3 minutes or until the eggs are just set. Place 4 rösti on each warmed serving plate, divide the roasted tomatoes between the plates and add a baked egg to each.

scrambled eggs with asparagus

Serves **2**
Preparation time **10 minutes**
Cooking time **5 minutes**

4 **large eggs**
4 tablespoons **single cream**
100 g (3½ oz) **asparagus spears**, woody ends removed
15 g (½ oz) **butter**
50 g (2 oz) **soft goats' cheese**, diced
4 slices of **brioche**, toasted
salt and **black pepper**

Beat the eggs and cream together in a bowl and season with salt and pepper.

Steam the asparagus spears for 4–5 minutes until tender.

Meanwhile, melt the butter in a small saucepan, add the egg mixture and cook over a low heat, stirring with a wooden spoon, until softly set. Remove from the heat and stir in the goats' cheese.

Serve the scrambled eggs on the toasted brioche with the steamed asparagus.

For cheese & watercress scrambled eggs, follow the recipe above to prepare and cook the scrambled eggs, then stir in 50 g (2 oz) grated mature Cheddar cheese, omitting the goats' cheese. Meanwhile, split 2 muffins, then toast and butter. Remove the scrambled eggs from the heat and stir in a large handful of chopped watercress. Divide the mixture between the muffins and serve immediately.

quinoa porridge with raspberries

Serves **2**
Preparation time **5 minutes**
Cooking time **25–30 minutes**

600 ml (1 pint) **milk**
100 g (3½ oz) **quinoa**
2 tablespoons **caster sugar**
½ teaspoon **ground cinnamon**
125 g (4 oz) **fresh raspberries**
2 tablespoons **mixed seeds**, such as sunflower, linseed, pumpkin and hemp
2 tablespoons **clear honey**

Bring the milk to the boil in a small saucepan. Add the quinoa and return to the boil. Reduce the heat to low, cover and simmer for about 15 minutes until three-quarters of the milk has been absorbed.

Stir the sugar and cinnamon into the pan, re-cover and cook for 8–10 minutes or until almost all the milk has been absorbed and the quinoa is tender.

Spoon the porridge into 2 bowls, then top with the raspberries, sprinkle over the seeds and drizzle with the honey. Serve immediately.

For quinoa & maple syrup pancakes, mix together a 225 g (7½ oz) pack precooked quinoa, 1 large lightly beaten egg, 125 g (4 oz) plain flour, 2 teaspoons baking powder, ½ teaspoon each of ground cinnamon and salt, 200 ml (7 fl oz) milk and 2 tablespoons maple syrup in a large bowl until well combined. Melt a little butter in a frying pan, add separate heaped tablespoonfuls of the batter and cook for 2–3 minutes on each side until golden brown. Serve with maple syrup and fresh berries.

banana & buttermilk pancakes

Serves **4**
Preparation time **10 minutes**
Cooking time **20 minutes**

125 g (4 oz) **plain flour**
pinch of **salt**
1 teaspoon **baking powder**
200 ml (7 fl oz) **buttermilk**
1 **egg**
2 small **bananas**, thinly sliced
1 tablespoon **vegetable oil**

To serve
1 **banana**, sliced
25 g (1 oz) **pecan nuts**,
   chopped
2 tablespoons **maple syrup**

Sift the flour, salt and baking powder together into a large bowl, then make a well in the centre.

Beat the buttermilk and egg together in a jug, add to the well and gradually beat in the flour mixture from around the sides to make a smooth batter. Stir in the sliced bananas.

Heat a large nonstick frying pan over a medium heat. Dip a scrunched-up piece of kitchen paper into the oil and use to wipe over the pan. Drop 3 large tablespoonfuls of the batter into the pan to make 3 pancakes, spreading the batter out slightly with the spoon. Cook for 2–3 minutes until bubbles start to appear on the surface and the underside is golden brown, then flip over and cook for a further 2 minutes. Transfer the pancakes to a baking sheet and keep warm in a low oven while you repeat with the remaining oil and batter.

Serve 3 pancakes per person, topped with the extra sliced banana, sprinkled with the chopped nuts and drizzled with the maple syrup.

For peanut butter & banana breakfast shakes, roughly chop 4 ripe bananas and place in a blender with 750 ml (1¼ pints) cold milk and 4 tablespoons crunchy peanut butter. Blend until smooth, then divide between 4 glasses and serve immediately.

fruit & nut bars

Makes **8**
Preparation time **10 minutes**
Cooking time **15 minutes**

100 g (3½ oz) **butter**
4 tablespoons **maple syrup**
2 tablespoons **soft light
  brown sugar**
150 g (5 oz) **jumbo oats**
100 g (3½ oz) **oatmeal**
50 g (2 oz) **mixed nuts**,
  chopped
150 g (5 oz) **mixed soft dried
  pitted fruit**, such as figs,
  dates, ready-to-eat apricots
  and cranberries, chopped
2 tablespoons **sunflower
  seeds**

Grease a 20 cm (8 inch) square nonstick baking tin lightly and line the base with nonstick baking paper.

Melt the butter, syrup and sugar together in a saucepan. Stir in all the remaining ingredients except the sunflower seeds, then press the mixture into the prepared tin.

Sprinkle over the sunflower seeds, then bake in a preheated oven, 200°C (400°F), Gas Mark 6, for 15 minutes or until golden. Cut into 8 bars and leave to cool.

For speedy flapjacks, grease a 20 cm (8 in) square nonstick baking tin lightly and line the base with nonstick baking paper. Melt 175 g (6 oz) unsalted butter with 175 g (6 oz) soft dark brown sugar in a saucepan. Remove from the heat and stir through 250 g (8 oz) jumbo oats. Press the mixture into the prepared tin and bake in a preheated oven, 180°C (350°F), Gas Mark 4, for 15 minutes. Cut into 12 bars and leave to cool.

starters & snacks

moroccan spiced chickpeas

Serves **4**
Preparation time **5 minutes**
Cooking time **35–40 minutes**

2 x 400 g (13 oz) cans
  chickpeas, drained
  and rinsed
1 tablespoon **olive oil**
1 tablespoon **rose**
  harissa paste
1 tablespoon **Moroccan** or
  Middle Eastern spice mix,
  such as baharat
½ teaspoon **salt**

Dry the chickpeas on kitchen paper to remove any excess water.

Mix all the remaining ingredients together in a large bowl. Add the chickpeas and toss in the spice mix to coat.

Spread the chickpeas out in a single layer on a rimmed baking sheet and roast in a preheated oven, 200°C (400°F), Gas Mark 6, for 35–40 minutes until a deep golden colour. Leave to cool before serving.

For Indian spiced roasted mixed nuts, place 1 tablespoon sunflower oil in a small bowl and stir in 1 tablespoon medium curry powder and 1 teaspoon cumin seeds. Add 250 g (8 oz) mixed raw unsalted nuts, such as cashew nuts, macadamia nuts and almonds, and turn to coat in the spice mix. Spread out in a single layer on a nonstick baking sheet and roast in a preheated oven, 180°C (350°F), Gas Mark 4, for 10 minutes, shaking once, until lightly golden. Remove from the oven, sprinkle with 1 teaspoon sea salt and leave to cool. Serve in bowls as a snack.

courgette & mint fritters

Serves **4**
Preparation time **10 minutes**
Cooking time **18 minutes**

3 **courgettes**, coarsely grated
4 **spring onions**, chopped
4 tablespoons chopped **mint**
125 g (4 oz) **self-raising flour**
2 **eggs**, lightly beaten
125 g (4 oz) **ricotta cheese**
olive oil, for frying
salt and **black pepper**
lemon-flavoured
　mayonnaise, to serve

Mix the courgettes, spring onions, mint and flour together in a large bowl, then stir in the eggs. Mix well, season with salt and pepper, then gently fold in the ricotta.

Heat a little oil in a large frying pan. Add 4 separate heaped tablespoonfuls of the batter, flatten slightly and cook for about 3 minutes on each side until golden. Transfer the fritters to a baking sheet and keep warm in a low oven while you repeat with the remaining batter, adding a little more oil to the pan as necessary.

Serve the fritters immediately with a spoonful of lemon-flavoured mayonnaise.

For feta & courgette fritters, follow the recipe above to make the fritters, using 125 g (4 oz) crumbled feta cheese in place of the ricotta. Cook as above and serve with ready-made fresh tomato salsa instead of the mayonnaise.

vegetable spring rolls

Makes **12**
Preparation time **25 minutes**
Cooking time **12–15 minutes**

6 sheets of **filo pastry**,
  defrosted if frozen
25g (1 oz) **butter**, melted
sweet chilli dipping sauce,
  to serve

Filling
100 g (3½ oz) **bean sprouts**
50 g (2 oz) **cabbage**,
  shredded
1 **carrot**, cut into thin strips
½ **red pepper**, cored,
  deseeded and thinly sliced
6 **spring onions**, thinly sliced
1 **garlic clove**, crushed
2.5 cm (1 inch) piece of
  fresh root ginger, peeled
  and grated
1 tablespoon **dark soy sauce**

Mix all the filling ingredients together in a large bowl.

Lay the sheets of filo pastry on top of one another in a pile on a chopping board and cut in half.

Brush the edges of 1 piece of filo with a little of the melted butter. Place some of the filling on the bottom edge. Fold in the ends and roll up. Repeat with the remaining filo and filling.

Place the rolls on a baking sheet and brush with melted butter. Bake in a preheated oven, 190°C (375°F), Gas Mark 5, for 12–15 minutes until golden. Serve hot with sweet chilli dipping sauce.

For spinach & ricotta filo tarts, brush 4 holes of a muffin tin with olive oil. Take 16 x 12 cm (5 inch) squares of filo pastry and brush 1 square with olive oil, then place another at an angle on top to produce a star shape and brush will a little more oil. Repeat with another 2 squares. Use the layered filo to line an oiled muffin hole. Repeat with the remaining filo squares. Place 125 g (4 oz) ricotta cheese in a small bowl and stir in 25 g (1 oz) grated Cheddar cheese, 1 lightly beaten egg and a pinch of grated nutmeg, then season well with salt and pepper. Stir in 100 g (3½ oz) chopped baby spinach leaves. Fill the tart cases with the ricotta mixture and bake in a preheated oven, 180°C (350°F), Gas Mark 4, for 25 minutes until golden.

cajun popcorn

Serves **6**
Preparation time **5 minutes**
Cooking time about **5 minutes**

2 tablespoons **corn oil**
100 g (3½ oz) **popping corn**
100 g (3½ oz) **salted butter**
2 tablespoons **Cajun spice mix**

Heat the oil in a saucepan until almost smoking and add the corn so that it forms a layer 1–2 grains deep. Cover and shake the pan so that the corn becomes coated in the oil. Reduce the heat to medium and leave to cook for about 2 minutes while the corn is popping.

Shake the pan carefully once the popping subsides, then leave to cook for a further few seconds. Once the popping quietens down again, turn off the heat so that the popcorn doesn't burn.

Meanwhile, place the butter and spice mix in a small saucepan and heat over a low heat, stirring frequently, until melted.

Transfer the popcorn to a large bowl, drizzle over the spiced butter and stir until all the popcorn is coated in the butter. Serve immediately.

For toffee popcorn, cook the popcorn as above. Meanwhile, place 50 g (2 oz) each of butter and soft light brown sugar with 3 tablespoons golden syrup in a saucepan. Stir together over a medium heat until the butter has melted and the sugar has dissolved. Place the popcorn in a large bowl, drizzle over the toffee sauce and stir until all the popcorn is coated in the sauce. Stop stirring when the sauce has cooled and is beginning to set. Leave until cool enough to eat.

roasted red pepper & walnut dip

Serves **4–6**
Preparation time **10 minutes**,
  plus cooling
Cooking time **10 minutes**

4 large **red peppers**
75 g (3 oz) **walnut pieces**
juice of 1 **lemon**
1 tablespoon **pomegranate
  molasses**
½ teaspoon **chilli paste**
1 tablespoon **olive oil**
salt and **black pepper**

To serve
pomegranate seeds
mint leaves
flatbreads (optional)

Cut each pepper into quarters and remove and discard the core and seeds. Place skin-side up under a preheated high grill and cook until the skin is blackened. Transfer to a food bag and leave until cool enough to handle.

Remove and discard the blackened skins from the peppers and place the pepper flesh on kitchen paper to remove the excess moisture.

Place the walnuts in a food processor and process until finely ground. Add all the remaining ingredients, then process until smooth.

Scrape the mixture into a bowl and season to taste with salt and pepper.

Serve garnished with pomegranate seeds and mint leaves, with warmed flatbreads, if liked.

For griddled haloumi, pomegranate & rocket salad, mix together 150 g (5 oz) pomegranate seeds, 1 deseeded and finely chopped small red chilli, ½ small red onion, finely chopped, 2 teaspoons pomegranate molasses, the finely grated rind and juice of 1 lime and 4 tablespoons chopped fresh coriander. Divide 100 g (3½ oz) rocket leaves between 4 bowls and add 125 g (4 oz) chopped roasted red pepper, either home prepared or from a jar. Heat a griddle pan or large frying pan over a medium-high heat. When hot, add 500 g (1 lb) sliced haloumi and cook, in batches, for about 1 minute on each side. Arrange the cheese over the rocket, then drizzle over the pomegranate seed mixture. Serve immediately.

japanese-style guacamole

Serves **4**
Preparation time **15 minutes**

2 ripe **avocados**
juice of 2 small **limes**
1–2 teaspoons **wasabi paste**,
  to taste
4 **spring onions**, finely
  chopped
1 tablespoon **sesame seeds**,
  toasted
1 teaspoon **Japanese
  rice mirin**
1 teaspoon finely chopped
  pickled ginger
sesame seeds, for sprinkling
prawn or **rice crackers**,
  to serve

Cut the avocados in half and remove and discard the stones. Peel off the skin and roughly chop the flesh. Place in a bowl and roughly mash with a fork.

Stir in the lime juice, wasabi, spring onions, sesame seeds and mirin.

Transfer to a serving bowl and scatter over the pickled ginger and sesame seeds. Serve immediately, with crackers for dipping.

For avocado & rice salad with wasabi dressing, place 200 g (7 oz) cooled freshly cooked basmati rice in a bowl and stir in 1 stoned, peeled and chopped avocado, 50 g (2 oz) thinly sliced radishes, 100 g (3½ oz) cooked soya beans and ½ cucumber, halved lengthways, deseeded and thinly sliced. Whisk together 1 tablespoon each of Japanese rice mirin and toasted sesame oil, 2 teaspoons lime juice and 1 teaspoon wasabi paste, season to taste with salt and pepper and then pour over the salad. Toss gently and serve immediately.

griddled greek-style sandwiches

Serves **2**
Preparation time **15 minutes**
Cooking time **4–6 minutes**

¼ small **red onion**,
  thinly sliced
8 **cherry tomatoes**, quartered
4 **pitted black olives**,
  chopped
5 cm (2 inch) piece of
  cucumber, deseeded and
  cut into small pieces
1 teaspoon **dried oregano**
50 g (2 oz) **feta cheese**,
  crumbled
1 teaspoon **lemon juice**
2 round **seeded pitta breads**
25 g (1 oz) **Cheddar cheese**,
  grated
olive oil, for brushing
black pepper

Mix the onion, tomatoes, olives, cucumber, oregano and feta together in a small bowl. Add the lemon juice, season to taste with pepper and gently mix.

Split each pitta bread in half horizontally. Divide the feta mixture between the bottom halves of the pitta breads, then add the Cheddar. Cover with the top halves of the pitta breads.

Brush a griddle pan with oil and heat over a medium heat. When hot, add the sandwiches, press down gently with a spatula and cook for 2–3 minutes on each side until golden and the cheese has melted. Serve immediately.

For Greek salad with toasted pitta croutons, cut 4 ripe tomatoes into wedges and place in a bowl with ½ cucumber, deseeded and chopped, ¼ red onion, thinly sliced, 8 Greek kalamata olives and 100 g (3½ oz) crumbled feta cheese. Whisk together 2 tablespoons extra virgin olive oil, 1 tablespoon lemon juice and 1 teaspoon dried oregano in a jug and season to taste with pepper. Pour over the salad and toss gently. Lightly toast 2 wholemeal pitta breads, then cut into croutons. Divide the salad between 2 plates and scatter over the croutons.

tandoori tofu bites

Serves **4**
Preparation time **15 minutes**,
 plus standing and marinating
Cooking time **20–25 minutes**

400 g (13 oz) **firm tofu**,
 drained
lemon wedges and **parsley**,
 to serve

Marinade
100 ml (3½ fl oz) **thick
 natural yogurt**
1 teaspoon peeled and grated
 fresh root ginger
1 **garlic clove**, crushed
1 tablespoon **tandoori masala**
1 teaspoon **garam masala**
1 teaspoon **ground coriander**
½ teaspoon **salt**
¼ teaspoon **ground turmeric**
2 tablespoons **lemon juice**

Place the tofu between 2 pieces of kitchen paper and set a chopping board or other weight on top. Leave to stand for at least 10 minutes to remove the excess water.

Remove the weight and kitchen paper, then cut the tofu into cubes.

Mix all the marinade ingredients together in a large non-metallic bowl and stir in the tofu. Cover and leave to marinate for 1 hour.

Place the tofu pieces on a lightly oiled nonstick baking sheet and cook in a preheated oven, 200°C (400°F), Gas Mark 6, for 20–25 minutes, turning halfway through the cooking time.

Serve the tofu cubes with cocktail sticks for skewering, lemon wedges and a parsley garnish.

For baked teriyaki tofu bites, follow the recipe above to remove the excess water from the tofu, then cut into cubes. For the marinade, mix together 2 tablespoons each of dark soy sauce and rice wine or dry sherry, 2 teaspoons peeled and chopped fresh root ginger, 1 teaspoon chopped garlic and 1 tablespoon each of soft light brown sugar and sesame seeds in a large non-metallic bowl. Stir in the tofu, cover and leave to marinate for 30 minutes. Cook the tofu as above, then serve on cocktail sticks, garnished with shredded spring onions.

smoky spanish tortilla

Serves **6–8**
Preparation time **10 minutes**
Cooking time **30–35 minutes**

2 tablespoons **olive oil**
1 large **onion**, thinly sliced
1 teaspoon **smoked paprika**,
    plus extra for sprinkling
450 g (14½ oz) **potatoes**,
    scrubbed and thickly sliced
6 **eggs**
salt and **black pepper**

Heat 1 tablespoon of the oil in a 20 cm (8 inch) nonstick frying pan with a flameproof handle and a lid, add the onion and smoked paprika and cook gently for 4–5 minutes until the onion has softened.

Add the potatoes and stir to coat in the onion and paprika mixture. Cover and cook for 15 minutes, turning once and shaking the pan from time to time, until tender.

Beat the eggs together in a large bowl and season with salt and pepper. Add the potato and onion mixture and mix thoroughly.

Heat the remaining oil in the frying pan, add the egg and potato mixture and cook over a low heat for 8–10 minutes, without stirring, until set.

Place the pan under a preheated high grill and cook for 2–3 minutes until the top of the tortilla is golden brown. Transfer to a board, sprinkle with a little extra smoked paprika and serve cut into wedges.

For saffron potato tortilla, place 1 teaspoon saffron threads in a small heatproof bowl, then cover with 1 tablespoon boiling water and leave to steep while you cook the onion as above, omitting the paprika, and then the potatoes. Beat the eggs with the saffron and its steeping liquid, then continue as above.

broad bean hummus

Serves **4**

Preparation time **20 minutes**

Cooking time **4 minutes**

400 g (13 oz) **podded fresh
or frozen broad beans**

1 **garlic clove**, crushed

grated rind and juice of
1 lemon

3 tablespoons **extra virgin
olive oil**

125 g (4 oz) **goats' cheese**

8 slices of **ciabatta**, toasted

salt and **black pepper**

watercress leaves, to garnish

Cook the broad beans in a saucepan of boiling water for 4 minutes until tender. Drain the beans, then refresh under cold running water and drain again. Slip the beans out of their grey skins, discarding the skins.

Place the beans in a food processor with the garlic and pulse until roughly chopped. Add the lemon rind and juice and then, with the motor running, trickle in the oil through the feed tube. Process until smooth and season to taste with salt and pepper.

Spread a little goats' cheese on each slice of toasted ciabatta, top with the hummus and serve garnished with watercress leaves.

For broad bean, mint & mozzarella salad, cook 200 g (7 oz) broad beans in boiling water and then refresh under cold running water and remove the skins as above. Place the beans in a large bowl and stir in the grated rind and juice of 1 lemon and 2 tablespoons each of chopped mint and olive oil. Cut 2 buffalo mozzarella balls in half and place each half in the centre of a serving plate. Spoon over the broad bean mixture and serve immediately with plenty of freshly ground black pepper and a few mint leaves.

pea & mint falafel with mint dip

Serves **4**

Preparation time **20 minutes**, plus chilling

Cooking time **5–7 minutes**

175 g (6 oz) **frozen peas**

400 g (13 oz) can **chickpeas**, drained and rinsed, then drained again well

25 g (1 oz) **fresh white breadcrumbs**

1 **garlic clove**, crushed

1 **red** or **green chilli**, deseeded and finely chopped

1 tablespoon **ground cumin**

1 teaspoon **ground coriander**

4 tablespoons chopped **mint**

1 teaspoon **baking powder**

1 **egg**, lightly beaten

2 tablespoons **sunflower oil**

salt and **black pepper**

wholemeal pitta breads, to serve

Mint dip

100 ml (3½ fl oz) **low-fat natural yogurt**

2 tablespoons chopped **mint**

¼ **cucumber**, finely chopped

Cook the peas in a saucepan of boiling water for 1 minute. Drain the peas, then refresh under cold running water and drain again thoroughly.

Place the peas in a food processor with the chickpeas, breadcrumbs, garlic, chilli, spices, mint and salt and pepper, then pulse until roughly chopped. Add the baking powder and egg and pulse until well combined.

Divide and shape the chickpea mixture into golf ball-sized balls, then flatten slightly. Cover and chill in the refrigerator for 30 minutes.

Heat the oil in a large frying pan, add the falafel and cook over a medium heat for 2–3 minutes on each side until golden. Remove from the pan and drain on kitchen paper.

Meanwhile, mix all the ingredients for the dip together in a small bowl and season to taste with salt and pepper.

Serve the falafel with the mint dip, along with warmed wholemeal pitta bread.

For chickpea falafel, place 2 x 400 g (13 oz) cans chickpeas, drained and rinsed, then drained again well, in a food processor with all the other ingredients for the falafel above, omitting the peas and using 2 tablespoons each of chopped flat leaf parsley and chopped fresh coriander in place of the mint. Continue as above.

refried bean quesadillas

Serves **2**
Preparation time **5 minutes**
Cooking time about **4–6 minutes**

200 g (7 oz) can **refried beans**
2 **spring onions**, chopped
50 g (2 oz) drained canned **sweetcorn**
1 tablespoon chopped **fresh coriander**
2 **soft corn tortillas**
3 tablespoons **ready-made fresh tomato salsa**, plus extra to serve
50 g (2 oz) **Cheddar** or **Monterey Jack cheese**, grated
olive oil, for brushing

Mix together the refried beans, spring onions, sweetcorn and coriander in a bowl.

Spread 1 tortilla with the bean mixture, top with the salsa and sprinkle over the cheese. Cover with the remaining tortilla.

Brush a large frying or griddle pan with oil and heat over a medium heat. When hot, add the quesadilla and cook over a medium heat for 2–3 minutes, pressing down with a spatula, until the cheese starts to melt.

Place a large plate over the pan and invert the quesadilla on to the plate. Return to the pan and cook on the other side for 2–3 minutes.

Remove from the pan and cut into wedges. Serve with tomato salsa.

For refried bean & cheese burritos, place 2 large soft corn tortillas in a single layer in an ovenproof dish. Mix together a 400 g (13 oz) can refried beans, 2 chopped spring onions, 100 q (3½ oz) each of drained canned sweetcorn and grated Cheddar or Monterey Jack cheese, 2 tablespoons chopped fresh coriander and 6 tablespoons ready-made fresh tomato salsa in a large bowl. Divide the mixture between the tortillas, placing it down the centre, and spoon over another 200 g (7 oz) fresh tomato salsa and 50 g (2 oz) grated Cheddar or Monterey Jack cheese. Bake in a preheated oven, 200°C (400°F), Gas Mark 6, for about 15 minutes until piping hot and the cheese is melted and bubbling.

veggie scotch eggs

Makes **4**
Preparation time **25 minutes**,
  plus cooling
Cooking time **10 minutes**

6 **eggs**
1 tablespoon **sunflower oil**,
  plus 1 litre (1¾ pints) for
  deep-frying
1 small **onion**, finely chopped
1 **carrot**, grated
400 g (13 oz) can **red kidney
  beans**, drained and rinsed,
  then drained again well
400 g (13 oz) can **chickpeas**,
  drained and rinsed, then
  drained again well
finely grated rind and juice of
  ½ **lemon**
1 tablespoon **garam masala**
1 tablespoon chopped **flat
  leaf parsley**
50 g (2 oz) **plain flour**
100 g (3½ oz) **fresh white
  breadcrumbs**
salt and **black pepper**
salad leaves, to serve

Cook 4 of the eggs in a saucepan of boiling water for 6 minutes. Drain, then cool under cold running water and drain again. Leave to cool completely and shell.

Meanwhile, heat the 1 tablespoon oil in a frying pan, add the onion and carrot and cook over a medium heat for 3–4 minutes until softened. Transfer to a large bowl.

Place the kidney beans, chickpeas, lemon rind and juice and garam masala in a food processor and process until smooth. Add to the onion and carrot with the parsley and mix together. Season to taste with salt and pepper.

Beat the remaining eggs together lightly in a small bowl. Tip the flour and breadcrumbs into 2 separate bowls. Mould one-quarter of the chickpea mixture around each egg. Coat in the flour, then the beaten egg and finally the breadcrumbs.

Heat the oil for deep-frying in a deep-fat fryer or deep saucepan to 180–190°C (350–375°F), or until a cube of bread browns in 60 seconds. Deep-fry the eggs for 2–3 minutes until golden. Remove with a slotted spoon and drain on kitchen paper. Serve warm or cold with mixed salad leaves.

For chilli tomato jam, to serve as an accompaniment, place 500 g (1 lb) halved tomatoes, a 2.5 cm (1 inch) piece of fresh root ginger, peeled and chopped, 2 crushed garlic cloves and 2 deseeded and chopped red chillies in a food processor and process until smooth. Transfer to a saucepan and add 250 g (8 oz) soft light brown sugar and 3 tablespoons red wine vinegar. Bring to a boil and simmer, stirring occasionally, for 30–35 minutes until thickened. Leave to cool.

hot haloumi with fattoush salad

Serves **2**
Preparation time **10 minutes**
Cooking time **2–4 minutes**

2 teaspoons **olive oil**
250 g (8 oz) **haloumi cheese**,
  thickly sliced
lemon wedges, to serve

Fattoush salad
75 g (3 oz) **red pepper**, cored,
  deseeded and finely sliced
75 g (3 oz) **yellow pepper**,
  cored, deseeded and
  finely sliced
75 g (3 oz) **cucumber**,
  chopped
75 g (3 oz) **spring onions**,
  finely chopped
2 tablespoons chopped **flat
  leaf parsley**
2 tablespoons chopped **mint**
2 tablespoons chopped **fresh
  coriander**

Dressing
1 teaspoon **crushed garlic**
2 tablespoons **olive oil** or
  flaxseed oil
4 tablespoons **lemon juice**
salt and **black pepper**

Heat the oil in a nonstick frying pan, add the haloumi and cook over a medium–high heat for 1–2 minutes on each side until golden brown. Remove from the pan and keep warm.

Place the peppers, cucumber, spring onions and herbs in a bowl and stir to combine.

Make the dressing. Mix the garlic with the oil and lemon juice and season to taste with salt and pepper.

Pour the dressing over the salad and toss lightly to mix. Serve with the warm haloumi and lemon wedges for squeezing over.

main meals

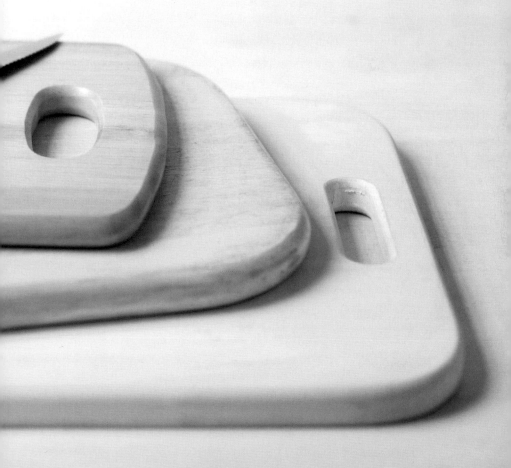

lentil & parsnip cottage pie

Serve **6**

Preparation time **20 minutes**

Cooking time **45 minutes**

1 tablespoon **sunflower oil**

1 large **onion**, chopped

2 **celery sticks**, finely sliced

4 **carrots**, chopped

250 g (8 oz) **chestnut mushrooms**, trimmed and chopped

2 x 400 g (13 oz) cans **green lentils in water**, drained

400 g (13 oz) can **chopped tomatoes**

1 tablespoon **tomato purée**

300 ml (½ pint) **vegetable stock**

2 teaspoons **dried mixed herbs**

500 g (1 lb) **parsnips**, peeled and chopped

500 g (1 lb) **floury potatoes**, peeled and chopped

2 tablespoons **milk**

25 g (1 oz) **butter**

50 g (2 oz) **mature Cheddar cheese**, grated

salt and **black pepper**

Heat the oil in a large saucepan, add the onion, celery and carrots and cook for 3–4 minutes until softened. Increase the heat, stir in the mushrooms and cook for a further 3 minutes, stirring occasionally.

Add the lentils, tomatoes, tomato purée and stock. Bring to the boil, then reduce the heat and simmer, uncovered, for 15 minutes. Season to taste with salt and pepper. Transfer to a 2 litre (3½ pint) ovenproof dish.

Meanwhile, cook the parsnips and potatoes in a large saucepan of lightly salted boiling water for 20 minutes or until tender.

Drain the root vegetables and return to the pan. Mash with the milk and butter, then season to taste with salt and pepper.

Spoon the parsnip mash over the lentil mixture and scatter over the cheese. Bake in a preheated oven, 190°C (375°F), Gas Mark 5, for 20 minutes until golden and bubbling.

For lentil pie with sweet potato & goats' cheese mash, prepare the lentil filling as above. Cook 1 kg (2 lb) sweet potatoes, peeled and chopped, in a large saucepan of boiling water for about 15 minutes or until tender. Drain, return to the pan and mash with the milk and butter as above. Stir in 50 g (2 oz) grated hard goats' cheese. Pile on top of the lentil mixture and bake as above.

beetroot & squash spaghetti

Serves **4**
Preparation time **10 minutes**
Cooking time **10 minutes**

300 g (10 oz) **dried spaghetti**
  or **fusilli**
150 g (5 oz) **fine green beans**
500 g (1 lb) **butternut
  squash**, peeled, deseeded
  and cut into 1 cm
  (½ inch) dice
4 tablespoons **olive oil**
500 g (1 lb) **raw beetroot**,
  peeled and cut into 1 cm
  (½ inch) dice
50 g (2 oz) **walnuts**, crushed
150 g (5 oz) **goats' cheese**,
  diced
2 tablespoons **lemon juice**
salt
vegetarian pasta cheese,
  to serve (optional)

Cook the pasta in a large saucepan of lightly salted boiling water for 10 minutes, or according to the packet instructions, until al dente. Add the beans and squash for the final 2 minutes of cooking time.

Meanwhile, heat the oil in a large frying pan, add the beetroot and cook, stirring occasionally, for 10 minutes until cooked but still firm.

Drain the pasta and vegetables, add to the frying pan and toss with the cooked beetroot, walnuts and goats' cheese.

Sprinkle over the lemon juice and serve immediately with a bowl of grated vegetarian pasta cheese, if liked.

For baby carrot & squash spaghetti, toss the butternut squash and 4 peeled garlic cloves in 4 tablespoons olive oil in a roasting tray and roast in a preheated oven, 240°C (475°F), Gas Mark 9, for about 40 minutes until softened. Meanwhile, cook the pasta as above. At the same time, cook 500 g (1 lb) baby carrots in a separate saucepan of boiling water for about 5 minutes until tender. Drain the pasta and carrots and return to the pasta pan. Add the roasted squash and garlic with 150 g (5 oz) diced havarti or dolcelatte cheese instead of the goats' cheese and toss well. Sprinkle over the lemon juice and serve hot.

red onion & goats' cheese tart

Serves **4**

Preparation time **15 minutes**,
plus cooling

Cooking time **40 minutes**

25 g (1 oz) **unsalted butter**

4 large **red onions**,
thinly sliced

1 teaspoon **soft light
brown sugar**

2 tablespoons chopped
thyme, plus a few extra
leaves to garnish

2 teaspoons **balsamic vinegar**

320 g (10½ oz) sheet of
ready-rolled puff pastry,
defrosted if frozen

2 x 100 g (3½ oz) round
goats' cheeses, each sliced
into 4

Melt the butter in a large frying pan, add the onions, sugar and chopped thyme and cook gently for 20 minutes, stirring occasionally, until the onions start to caramelize. Stir in the vinegar and cook for 1 minute. Leave to cool slightly.

Unroll the pastry sheet and place on a nonstick baking sheet. Using a sharp knife, score a line along each side of the sheet 2.5 cm (1 inch) from the edge, being careful not to cut all the way through the pastry.

Spoon the caramelized onions over the pastry, within the scored border, then top with the goats' cheese slices.

Bake in a preheated oven, 200°C (400°F), Gas Mark 6, for 20 minutes until the pastry is risen and golden. Serve garnished with a few thyme leaves.

For ricotta & cherry tomato tart, prepare the puff pastry base as above. Beat together 250 g (8 oz) ricotta cheese, 25 g (1 oz) finely grated Cheddar cheese, 2 large eggs and 2 tablespoons shredded basil in a bowl until well combined. Season with a little salt and pepper. Spoon the mixture over the pastry, within the scored border, then top with 250 g (8 oz) halved cherry tomatoes. Bake as above.

feta, herb & rocket frittata

Serves **2**
Preparation time **5 minutes**
Cooking time **8–10 minutes**

4 **eggs**, beaten
2 tablespoons chopped **fresh
   herbs**, such as chives,
   chervil and parsley
1 tablespoon **double cream**
1 tablespoon **olive oil**
1 small **red onion**, finely sliced
½ **red pepper**, cored,
   deseeded and finely sliced
100 g (3½ oz) **feta cheese**
large handful of **rocket leaves**
salt and **black pepper**

Beat the eggs, herbs and cream together in a bowl, and season with salt and pepper.

Heat the oil in a nonstick frying pan with a flameproof handle, add the onion and red pepper and cook over a medium heat for 3–4 minutes until just softened.

Pour in the egg mixture and cook for about 3 minutes until almost set, then crumble over the feta.

Place the pan under a preheated high grill and cook for 2–3 minutes until the top of the tortilla is golden brown. Top with the rocket and serve.

For potato & goats' cheese frittata, beat the eggs, herbs and cream together, then season as above. Add 150 g (5 oz) cooked and sliced new potatoes to the egg mixture and cook as above. Arrange 4 slices of firm goats' cheese over the frittata and finish cooking under a preheated high grill. Serve with a large handful of rocket leaves.

pasta with fennel & rocket

Serves **2**
Preparation time **10 minutes**
Cooking time **15 minutes**

1 tablespoon **olive oil**
1 **fennel bulb**, trimmed and
 thinly sliced
1 **garlic clove**, chopped
100 ml (3½ fl oz) **dry**
 white wine
4 tablespoons **crème fraîche**
grated rind and juice of 1 small
 lemon
50 g (2 oz) **rocket leaves**
250 g (8 oz) **fresh tagliatelle**
 or **pappardelle**
salt and **black pepper**
grated **vegetarian pasta**
 cheese, to serve

Heat the oil in a frying pan, add the fennel and garlic and cook gently for about 10 minutes until the fennel is soft and golden.

Add the wine to the pan and cook until reduced by half. Stir in the crème fraîche, lemon rind and juice and rocket and cook, stirring, until the rocket has wilted. Season to taste with salt and pepper.

Meanwhile, cook the pasta in a large saucepan of lightly salted boiling water for 3–4 minutes, or according to the packet instructions, until al dente. Drain and return to the pan.

Stir the sauce into the cooked pasta and toss well. Season with freshly ground black pepper and serve immediately with the cheese.

For penne with fennel, chilli & basil, heat 3 tablespoons olive oil in a frying pan, add 2 crushed garlic cloves and a pinch of dried chilli flakes and cook, stirring, for 1 minute. Add 1 trimmed and thinly sliced fennel bulb and cook gently for about 10 minutes until soft and golden. Meanwhile, cook 250 g (8 oz) fresh penne in a large saucepan of lightly salted boiling water for 3–4 minutes, or according to the packet instructions, until al dente. Drain, reserving 2 tablespoons of the cooking water, and return to the pan. Add the fennel mixture and the reserved cooking water and stir well, then toss in 1 tablespoon shredded basil leaves. Serve immediately, sprinkled with 2 tablespoons grated vegetarian pasta cheese.

spinach & potato gratin

Serves **4**
Preparation time **10 minutes**
Cooking time **35 minutes**

625 g (1¼ lb) **potatoes**,
  peeled and thinly sliced
500 g (1 lb) **spinach leaves**
200 g (7 oz) **mozzarella
  cheese**, grated
4 **tomatoes**, sliced
3 **eggs**, beaten
300 ml (½ pint) **whipping
  cream**
salt and **black pepper**

Cook the potatoes in a large saucepan of salted boiling water for 5 minutes, then drain well.

Meanwhile, cook the spinach in a separate saucepan of boiling water for 1–2 minutes. Drain and squeeze out the excess water.

Grease a large ovenproof dish and line the bottom with half the potato slices. Cover with the spinach and half the mozzarella, seasoning each layer well with salt and pepper. Cover with the remaining potato slices and arrange the tomato slices on top. Scatter with the remaining mozzarella.

Beat the eggs and cream together in a bowl and season well with salt and pepper. Pour over the ingredients in the dish.

Bake in a preheated oven, 180°C (350°F), Gas Mark 4, for about 30 minutes. Serve immediately.

For tomato, lime & basil salad, to serve as an accompaniment, slice or quarter 1 kg (2 lb) tomatoes while the gratin is baking, then arrange in a large serving bowl. Scatter over ½ red onion, thinly sliced, and a handful of basil leaves. Whisk together 4 tablespoons olive oil, 2 tablespoons chopped basil, 1 tablespoon lime juice, 1 teaspoon grated lime rind, ½ teaspoon clear honey, 1 crushed garlic clove, a pinch of cayenne pepper and salt and pepper to taste. Pour over the salad. Cover and leave to stand at room temperature for about 30 minutes to allow the flavours to mingle, then serve with the gratin.

mexican bean burgers

Serves **4**

Preparation time **15 minutes**, plus cooling

Cooking time **12–15 minutes**

1 tablespoon **sunflower oil**
1 **onion**, finely chopped
1 **green chilli**, deseeded and finely chopped
2 teaspoons **Mexican** or **fajita spice mix**
2 x 400 g (13 oz) cans **red kidney beans**, drained and rinsed
100 g (3½ oz) **fresh white breadcrumbs**
4 tablespoons chopped **fresh coriander**
1 **egg**
2 teaspoons **chipotle paste**
salt and black pepper

To serve
4 **burger buns**
crisp green lettuce
ready-made fresh tomato salsa
ready-made guacamole

Heat the oil in a small frying pan, add the onion and chilli and cook over a medium heat for 2–3 minutes until softened. Stir in the spice mix and cook, stirring, for 1 minute. Leave to cool slightly.

Mash the beans in a large bowl with a potato masher or fork, then add the breadcrumbs and coriander and season well with salt and pepper.

Beat the egg with the paste in a jug, then add to the bean mixture and mix together well with a fork.

Divide the bean mixture into 4 and shape each portion into a burger.

Place the burgers on a nonstick baking sheet and cook under a preheated medium-high grill for 4–5 minutes on each side until golden and cooked through.

Split the buns in half horizontally. Top the bottom halves of the buns with some lettuce and a spoonful of salsa. Place the burgers on top and finish with a spoonful of guacamole. Cover with the top halves of the buns.

For spicy Mexican meatballs, prepare the bean mixture as above, then shape into 16–18 balls. Heat 1 tablespoon sunflower oil in a large frying pan, add the meatballs and cook for 4–5 minutes, turning occasionally. Pour over 500 ml (17 fl oz) passata (sieved tomatoes) and add 1 teaspoon each of dried oregano and granulated sugar. Cover and simmer for 10 minutes. Serve with rice and a spoonful of soured cream.

golden mushroom & leek pies

Serves **4**
Preparation time **15 minutes**
Cooking time **25–30 minutes**

25 g (1 oz) **butter**
2 **leeks**, trimmed, cleaned and
  thinly sliced
300 g (10 oz) **chestnut**
  mushrooms, trimmed
  and quartered
300 g (10 oz) **button**
  mushrooms, trimmed
  and quartered
1 tablespoon **plain flour**
250 ml (8 fl oz) **milk**
150 ml (¼ pint) **double cream**
100 g (3½ oz) **strong**
  Cheddar cheese, grated
4 tablespoons finely chopped
  parsley
2 sheets of **ready-rolled puff**
  pastry, defrosted if frozen
beaten egg, to glaze

Melt the butter in a large saucepan, add the leeks and cook over a medium heat for 1–2 minutes. Add the mushrooms and cook for 2 minutes.

Stir in the flour and cook, stirring, for 1 minute, then gradually add the milk and cream and cook, stirring constantly, until the sauce boils and thickens. Add the Cheddar and parsley and cook, stirring, for 1–2 minutes. Remove from the heat.

Cut 4 rounds from the pastry sheets to cover 4 individual pie dishes. Divide the mushroom mixture between the pie dishes. Brush the rims with the beaten egg, then place the pastry rounds on top. Press down around the rims and crimp the edges with a fork. Cut a couple of slits in the top of each pie to let the steam out. Brush the pastry with the remaining beaten egg.

Bake in a preheated oven, 220°C (425°F), Gas Mark 7, for 15–20 minutes until the pastry is golden brown. Serve hot.

spiced tofu, noodles & pak choi

Serves **4**
Preparation time **10 minutes**,
plus standing
Cooking time **10 minutes**

300 g (10 oz) **firm tofu**,
drained
250 g (8 oz) **dried medium
egg noodles**
1 tablespoon **cornflour**
½ teaspoon **salt**
1 teaspoon **ground
black pepper**
½ teaspoon **Chinese five-
spice powder**
2 tablespoons **sunflower oil**
2.5 cm (1 inch) piece of **fresh
root ginger**, peeled and
finely chopped
1 tablespoon **dark soy sauce**
2 tablespoons **sweet
chilli sauce**
100 ml (3½ fl oz) **water**
2 heads of **pak choi**, trimmed
and leaves separated to
the pan

Place the tofu between 2 pieces of kitchen paper and set a chopping board or other weight on top. Leave to stand for at least 10 minutes to remove excess water.

Remove the weight and kitchen paper, then cut the tofu into cubes.

Cook the noodles according to the packet instructions. Drain and set aside.

Mix together the cornflour, salt, pepper and five-spice powder in a bowl and use to coat the tofu. Heat 1 tablespoon of the oil in a wok or large frying pan over a high heat. Add the tofu and stir-fry for 2–3 minutes until golden. Remove from the pan and keep warm.

Heat the remaining oil in the pan, add the ginger and stir-fry for 1 minute. Add the noodles, stir in the soy sauce, chilli sauce and measurement water, then add the pak choi. Cook, stirring, until the leaves start to wilt.

Divide the noodles between plates and top with the tofu.

For stir-fried tofu with hoisin sauce, prepare and stir-fry the tofu as above, omitting the coating. Remove from the pan and keep warm. Add 1 crushed garlic clove and 2 teaspoons chopped fresh ginger to the pan and stir-fry for 1 minute. Add 250 g (8 oz) trimmed Tenderstem broccoli, 150 g (5 oz) halved mangetout and 1 bunch of spring onions, chopped, and stir-fry for 2–3 minutes, then stir in 25 g (1 oz) toasted cashew nuts, 2 tablespoons hoisin sauce and 2 tablespoons water and 1 tablespoon soy sauce. Return the tofu to the pan and simmer for 1 minute to heat through.

mushroom & spinach lasagne

Serves **4**
Preparation time **15 minutes**
Cooking time **10 minutes**

3 tablespoons **extra virgin olive oil**
500 g (1 lb) **mixed mushrooms**, trimmed and sliced
200 g (7 oz) **mascarpone cheese**
12 sheets of **fresh lasagne**
150 g (5 oz) **Taleggio cheese**, rind removed and cut into cubes
125 g (4 oz) **baby spinach leaves**
salt and **black pepper**

Heat the oil in a large frying pan, add the mushrooms and cook over a medium heat for 5 minutes. Add the mascarpone and cook over a high heat for 1 minute until thickened. Season to taste with salt and pepper.

Meanwhile, put the pasta sheets in a large roasting tray and cover with boiling water. Leave to stand for about 5 minutes until tender, then drain.

Brush an ovenproof dish lightly with oil and place 3 pasta sheets over the base, slightly overlapping. Top the pasta with a little of the Taleggio, one-third of the mushroom sauce and one-third of the spinach. Repeat the process with 2 more layers, then top the final layer of pasta with the remaining Taleggio.

Place the dish under a preheated high grill and cook for 5 minutes until the cheese is golden brown. Serve immediately.

For mushroom, tomato & courgette lasagne, use 500 g (1 lb) tomatoes and 2 courgettes in place of the spinach. Blanch the tomatoes in a saucepan of boiling water, then skin and slice, and thinly slice the courgettes, before proceeding with the recipe, as above.

root vegetable & bean crumble

Serves **4–6**
Preparation time **20 minutes**
Cooking time **50–55 minutes**

1 tablespoon **olive oil**
2 **carrots**, sliced
2 **parsnips**, peeled and
  chopped
2 **leeks**, trimmed, cleaned
  and sliced
300 ml (½ pint) **red wine**
400 g (13 oz) can **chopped
  tomatoes**
300 ml (½ pint) **vegetable
  stock**
400 g (13 oz) can **butter
  beans**, drained and rinsed
1 tablespoon chopped
  rosemary
salt and **black pepper**

Crumble topping
100 g (3½ oz) sliced
  wholemeal bread, roughly
  torn into pieces
50 g (2 oz) **walnuts**,
  roughly chopped
2 tablespoons chopped **flat
  leaf parsley**
100 g (3½ oz) **Wensleydale**
  or **Lancashire cheese**,
  crumbled

Heat the oil in a large saucepan, add the carrots, parsnips and leeks and cook over a medium heat for 4–5 minutes until slightly softened.

Stir the wine into the pan and cook until reduced by half, then stir in the tomatoes, stock, butter beans and rosemary. Season well with salt and pepper, then cover and simmer for 15 minutes, stirring occasionally. Transfer to a 2 litre (3½ pint) ovenproof dish.

Meanwhile, make the crumble topping. Place the bread, walnuts, parsley and 75 g (3 oz) of the cheese in a food processor and pulse until the mixture resembles breadcrumbs.

Spoon the topping over the vegetable mixture and scatter over the remaining cheese. Bake in a preheated oven, 180°C (350°F), Gas Mark 4, for 25–30 minutes until golden and crisp. Serve immediately with steamed green vegetables, if liked.

For butter bean & root vegetable pie, prepare the root vegetable filling as above and place in the ovenproof dish. Reheat 2 x 450 g (14½ oz) packs fresh mashed potatoes according to the packet instructions and spoon over the top of the vegetable mixture. Sprinkle over 100 g (3½ oz) grated mature Cheddar cheese and bake as above for 15–20 minutes until the topping is golden.

spring vegetable & herb pilaf

Serves **4**
Preparation time **15 minutes**
Cooking time **20 minutes**

2 tablespoons **extra virgin
   olive oil**
1 **leek**, trimmed, cleaned
   and sliced
1 **courgette**, diced
grated rind and juice of
   1 **lemon**
2 **garlic cloves**, crushed
300 g (10 oz) **white long-
   grain rice**
600 ml (1 pint) **hot vegetable
   stock**
150 g (5 oz) **green beans**,
   topped and tailed and
   chopped
150 g (5 oz) **fresh** or
   frozen peas
4 tablespoons chopped **mixed
   herbs**, such as mint, parsley
   and chives
50 g (2 oz) **flaked almonds**,
   toasted
salt and **black pepper**

Heat the olive oil in a large frying pan, add the leek, courgette, lemon rind, garlic and a little salt and pepper and cook gently for 5 minutes.

Add the rice, stir once and pour in the hot stock. Bring to the boil, then reduce the heat, cover and simmer gently for 10 minutes.

Stir in the beans and peas, cover and cook for a further 5 minutes.

Remove the pan from the heat and leave to stand for 5 minutes. Stir in the lemon juice and herbs and serve scattered with the flaked almonds.

For winter vegetable & fruit pilaf, heat 2 table-spoons extra virgin olive oil in a large frying pan, add 1 sliced red onion, 1 teaspoon ground coriander and 2 teaspoons chopped thyme and cook gently for 5 minutes. Add 375 g (12 oz) diced pumpkin flesh with the rice as above, stir once and pour in the hot stock. Bring to the boil, then reduce the heat, cover and simmer gently for 10 minutes. Stir in 75 g (3 oz) raisins with the peas as above, cover and cook for 5 minutes. Remove the pan from the heat and leave to stand for 5 minutes. Stir in 2 tablespoons chopped fresh coriander with the lemon juice and almonds.

macaroni cheese with spinach

Serves **4**
Preparation time **10 minutes**
Cooking time **30 minutes**

300 g (10 oz) **dried macaroni**
350 g (11½ oz) **baby
spinach leaves**
50 g (2 oz) **butter**
50 g (2 oz) **plain flour**
750 ml (1¼ pints) **milk**
150 g (5 oz) **Taleggio** or
fontina cheese, chopped
2 teaspoons **wholegrain
mustard**
1 teaspoon **Dijon mustard**
8 **cherry tomatoes**, halved
50 g (2 oz) **fresh white
breadcrumbs**
25 g (2 oz) **Cheddar cheese**,
finely grated
salt and **black pepper**

Cook the macaroni in a large saucepan of lightly salted boiling water for 8–10 minutes, or according to the packet instructions, until al dente.

Add the spinach to the pan and cook for 1 minute until wilted. Drain well and place in a 1.5 litre (2½ pint) ovenproof dish.

Meanwhile, place the butter, flour and milk in a saucepan and whisk constantly over a medium heat until the sauce boils and thickens. Simmer for 2–3 minutes until you have a smooth glossy sauce, then reduce the heat to low and stir in the Taleggio or fontina and mustards. Season to taste with salt and pepper and cook gently until the cheese has melted.

Pour the sauce over the macaroni and spinach, scatter over the tomatoes and then sprinkle with the breadcrumbs and Cheddar.

Bake in a preheated oven, 200°C (400°F), Gas Mark 6, for 20 minutes until golden and bubbling.

For macaroni cheese with broccoli & cauliflower, cook the macaroni as above, steaming 300 g (10 oz) small broccoli and cauliflower florets above the pan for 5 minutes until tender. Drain the pasta and vegetables well and place in a 1.5 litre (2½ pint) ovenproof dish. Make the cheese sauce as above and pour over the macaroni and vegetables. Sprinkle with the breadcrumbs and Cheddar and bake as above until golden and bubbling.

spicy goan aubergine curry

Serves **4**
Preparation time **15 minutes**
Cooking time about **25
   minutes**

4 teaspoons **coriander seeds**
1 teaspoon **cumin seeds**
1 teaspoon **cayenne pepper**
2 **green chillies**, deseeded
   and sliced
½ teaspoon **ground turmeric**
4 **garlic cloves**, crushed
1 tablespoon peeled and
   grated **fresh root ginger**
300 ml (½ pint) **warm water**
400 ml (14 fl oz) **reduced-fat
   coconut milk**
1 tablespoon **tamarind paste**
1 large **aubergine**, thinly sliced
   lengthways
salt and **black pepper**
naan bread, or **chapatis**,
   to serve

Toast the coriander and cumin seeds in a dry frying pan over a medium heat until aromatic, then crush lightly with a pestle and mortar.

Place the crushed spices in a large saucepan with the cayenne, chillies, turmeric, garlic, ginger and the measurement water. Bring to the boil, then reduce the heat and simmer for 10 minutes until thickened. Season to taste with salt and pepper and stir in the coconut milk and tamarind paste.

Arrange the aubergine slices in a grill pan lined with foil and brush the tops with some of the curry sauce. Cook under a preheated high grill, turning once, until golden and tender.

Serve the aubergine slices in the curry sauce with naan bread or chapatis.

For cashew & courgette curry, prepare the curry sauce as above and add 200 g (7 oz) toasted cashew nuts to the finished sauce. To toast, soak in water for 20 minutes, then drain and chop. Heat in a dry frying pan over a medium heat, shaking frequently, until lightly browned. Continue with the recipe as above, using 4 sliced courgettes in place of the aubergine. Drizzle the finished dish with walnut oil and season with salt and pepper.

asparagus, mint & lemon risotto

Serves **4**
Preparation time **10 minutes**
Cooking time **25–30 minutes**

2 bunches of **asparagus spears** (about 500 g/1 lb), woody ends removed
1 **vegetable stock cube**
25 g (1 oz) **butter**
1 tablespoon **olive oil**
1 **onion**, chopped
300 g (10 oz) **risotto rice**
150 ml (¼ pint) **dry white wine**
grated rind and juice of 1 **lemon**
4 tablespoons chopped **mint**
50 g (2 oz) **vegetarian pasta cheese**, grated, plus extra to serve

Chop the asparagus stalks finely, leaving the tips whole. Cook the asparagus tips and stalks in a saucepan of simmering water for about 3 minutes until al dente. Drain, reserving the cooking water.

Pour the reserved cooking water over the stock cube in a measuring jug, make up to 900 ml (1½ pints) with boiling water and stir to dissolve the cube.

Meanwhile, melt the butter with the oil in a saucepan, add the onion and cook over a medium heat for about 2 minutes, until softened. Stir in the rice and cook for 1 minute, stirring, until well coated in the onion mixture.

Pour in the wine and cook for 2–3 minutes until absorbed. Gradually add the hot stock, 125 ml (4 fl oz) at a time, stirring constantly and cooking until most of the liquid has been absorbed before adding the next batch of stock. Continue until almost all of the stock has been absorbed and the rice is creamy but still firm. This will take about 15 minutes.

Stir in the asparagus tips and stalks and cook for 2–3 minutes until heated through. Stir in the lemon rind and juice, mint and cheese. Cover and leave to stand for about 1 minute. Serve in bowls with extra grated cheese for sprinkling.

For asparagus & goats' cheese risotto, follow the recipe above to prepare the risotto, omitting the mint and cheese and stirring 125 g (4 oz) chopped creamy goats' cheese and 2 tablespoons chopped parsley into the cooked risotto. Cover and leave to stand for about 1 minute before serving.

courgette & creamy tomato penne

Serves **4**
Preparation time **10 minutes**
Cooking time **12 minutes**

1 tablespoon **olive oil**
1 **onion**, chopped
1 **garlic clove**, finely chopped
3 **courgettes**, chopped
1 **red pepper**, cored,
    deseeded and chopped
200 g (7 oz) **mascarpone
    cheese**
200 ml (7 fl oz) **passata**
    (sieved tomatoes)
2 tablespoons chopped **basil**
500 g (1 lb) **fresh penne**
salt and **black pepper**

Heat the oil in a frying pan, add the onion and garlic and cook over a medium heat for 3 minutes until softened. Stir in the courgettes and red pepper and cook for 5 minutes until the courgettes have softened.

Stir the mascarpone into the pan until melted, then add the passata and simmer for 2–3 minutes. Season to taste with salt and pepper and stir in the basil.

Meanwhile, cook the pasta in a large saucepan of lightly salted boiling water for 3–4 minutes, or according to the packet instructions, until al dente. Drain and return to the pan.

Stir the sauce into the cooked pasta and toss well. Serve immediately with the basil scattered over.

For gnocchi with creamy tomato sauce, cook 500 g (1 lb) chilled fresh gnocchi in a large saucepan of boiling water for 2–3 minutes, or according to the packet instructions, until they rise to the surface, then drain. Meanwhile, gently heat the passata (sieved tomatoes) in a saucepan and stir in the mascarpone cheese until melted. Simmer for 2–3 minutes, then stir in 200 g (7 oz) baby spinach leaves until wilted. Stir the cooked gnocchi into the sauce, season with pepper and serve immediately with grated vegetarian pasta cheese.

leek & chestnut patties

Serves **4**
Preparation time **20 minutes**
Cooking time **15 minutes**

875 g (1¾ lb) **swede**, peeled
and diced
3–4 tablespoons **semi-skimmed milk**
375 g (12 oz) **leeks**, trimmed,
cleaned and finely chopped
50 g (2 oz) **soft pitted prunes**,
finely chopped
50 g (2 oz) **Brazil nuts**,
roughly chopped
240 g (7½ oz) can **whole peeled chestnuts**, crumbled
125 g (4 oz) **fresh white breadcrumbs**
1 **egg**, lightly beaten
3 tablespoons **sunflower oil**
salt and **black pepper**
parsley sprigs, to garnish

Cranberry sauce
2 teaspoons **cornflour**
200 ml (7 fl oz) **vegetable stock**
2 tablespoons **cranberry sauce**
1 tablespoon **red wine vinegar**
1 teaspoon **Dijon mustard**
1 teaspoon **tomato purée**

Cook the swede in a saucepan of boiling water for 15 minutes until tender. Drain and return to the pan. Mash with the milk, season to taste with salt and pepper and keep warm.

Meanwhile, mix together the leeks, prunes, Brazil nuts and chestnuts in a large bowl. Mix in the breadcrumbs, egg and salt and pepper. Shape the mixture into 16 patties with lightly floured hands.

Heat the oil in a frying pan, add the patties and cook over a medium heat for 10 minutes, turning several times, until browned and heated through.

Make the sauce. Mix the cornflour with a little water in a small bowl until smooth. Place the remaining sauce ingredients in a jug, add the cornflour mixture and stir.

Push the patties to one side of the pan, add the sauce mixture and bring to the boil, stirring constantly, until thickened.

Spoon the swede mash on to warmed plates and top with the patties and sauce. Garnish with the parsley and serve.

tikka lentil koftas

Serves **4**
Preparation time **20 minutes**
Cooking time **12–15 minutes**

3 tablespoons **sunflower oil**
1 **onion**, finely chopped
1 **garlic clove**, crushed
1 teaspoon peeled and
chopped **fresh root ginger**
1 **green chilli**, deseeded and
finely chopped
2 tablespoons **tikka curry
paste**
grated rind and juice of
½ **lemon**
2 x 400 g (13 oz) cans **green
lentils**, drained and rinsed
2 tablespoons chopped **fresh
coriander**
25 g (1 oz) **fresh white
breadcrumbs**
plain flour, for coating
1 large **egg**, lightly beaten
75 g (3 oz) **dried natural
breadcrumbs**
salt and **black pepper**

To serve
raita
green salad leaves

Heat 1 tablespoon of the oil in a large saucepan, add the onion, garlic, ginger and chilli and cook over a medium heat for 3–4 minutes until softened. Stir in the curry paste and lemon rind and juice and cook, stirring, for 1 minute.

Remove the pan from the heat and stir in the lentils, coriander and fresh breadcrumbs, then season well with salt and pepper. Mix well, mashing with a spoon so that the mixture holds together.

Divide the mixture into 8 equal portions, using slightly wet hands. Flatten slightly, then roll in the flour. Place the beaten egg and dried breadcrumbs in separate dishes. Dip each kofta in the egg and then in the breadcrumbs until coated.

Heat the remaining oil in a large saucepan, add the koftas and fry over a medium heat for 4–5 minutes on each side until crisp and golden. Serve with a cucumber and mint raita and crisp green salad.

For lentil & spinach tikka, cook the onion, garlic, ginger and chilli as above, then stir in the curry paste and lemon rind and juice and cook, stirring, for 1 minute. Add the lentils with a 400 g (13 oz) can chopped tomatoes and 150 ml (¼ pint) vegetable stock. Simmer for 10–15 minutes until thickened. Stir in 250 g (8 oz) baby spinach leaves and cook until just wilted. Stir in 2 tablespoons chopped fresh coriander and serve hot with naan bread.

orecchiette with walnut sauce

Serves **4**
Preparation time **5 minutes**
Cooking time **11–13 minutes**

375 g (12 oz) **dried
  orecchiette**
50 g (2 oz) **butter**
15 **sage leaves**, roughly
  chopped
2 **garlic cloves**, finely chopped
125 g (4 oz) **walnuts**, finely
  chopped
150 ml (¼ pint) **single cream**
65 g (2½ oz) **vegetarian
  pasta cheese**, grated
salt and **black pepper**

Cook the pasta in a large saucepan of lightly salted boiling water for 11–13 minutes, or according to the packet instructions, until al dente.

Meanwhile, melt the butter in a frying pan over a medium heat. When it begins to foam and sizzle, stir in the sage and garlic and cook, stirring, for 1–2 minutes until golden. Remove from the heat and stir in the walnuts, cream and cheese.

Drain the pasta and stir it thoroughly into the sauce. Season to taste with salt and pepper and serve immediately.

For spinach, spring onion & avocado salad, to serve as an accompaniment, place 150 g (5 oz) baby spinach leaves, 4 finely sliced spring onions and 2 stoned, peeled and sliced avocados in a large bowl and toss together. Spoon into separate side dishes.

oven-baked squash with quinoa

Serves **4**
Preparation time **10 minutes**
Cooking time **40 minutes**

2 tablespoons **olive oil**
750 g (1½ lb) **butternut
    squash**, peeled, deseeded
    and cut into 3.5 cm
    (1½ inch) chunks
25 g (1 oz) **unsalted butter**
1 **red onion**, chopped
1 **garlic clove**, crushed
50 g (2 oz) **pine nuts**
300 g (10 oz) **quinoa**
150 ml (¼ pint) **dry white
    wine**
1 **cinnamon stick**
1 litre (1¾ pints) **vegetable
    stock**
4 tablespoons chopped **mint**
200 g (7 oz) **feta cheese**,
    crumbled
100 g (3½ oz) **pomegranate
    seeds**
salt and **black pepper**

Heat the oil in a large frying pan and add the squash in a single layer. Season well with salt and pepper and cook over a medium heat for about 10 minutes until lightly browned.

Meanwhile, melt the butter in a flameproof casserole dish, add the onion and garlic and cook for 2–3 minutes until softened. Stir in the pine nuts and quinoa and cook for 1 minute or until the quinoa is starting to pop. Add the wine and cook until it has been absorbed.

Stir in the squash, cinnamon stick and stock. Bring to the boil, season to taste with salt and pepper and stir well.

Cover the dish with the lid and cook in a preheated oven, 190°C (375°F), Gas Mark 5, for 25 minutes until the quinoa is just tender.

Stir in the mint, then scatter over the feta and pomegranate seeds. Serve immediately.

oriental mushroom parcels

Makes **4**
Preparation time **25 minutes**
Cooking time **25 minutes**

4 large **field mushrooms**
1 tablespoon **sesame oil**
1 tablespoon **ketjap manis** or
   soy sauce
2.5 cm (1 inch) piece of **fresh
   root ginger**, peeled and
   finely chopped
2 **garlic cloves**, finely chopped
4 tablespoons roughly
   chopped **fresh coriander**
1 **tomato**, cut into 4 thick
   slices
25 g (1 oz) **butter**, cut into
   4 pieces
475 g (15 oz) **ready-made
   shortcrust pastry**, defrosted
   if frozen
beaten egg, to glaze
4 teaspoons **sesame seeds**
black pepper

Trim the top of the mushroom stalks level with the caps, drizzle the gills with the sesame oil and ketjap manis or soy sauce and then sprinkle with the ginger, garlic and coriander. Top each with a slice of tomato, a piece of butter and a little pepper.

Cut the pastry into 4 pieces, roll out one piece thinly on a lightly floured surface to a roughly shaped 18–20 cm (7–8 inch) round, or large enough to enclose the mushrooms (this will depend on how big they are, so make a little larger if needed).

Place a mushroom on top of each pastry round, brush the edges with beaten egg, then lift the pastry up and over the top of the mushroom, pleating the pastry as you go and pinching the ends together in the centre of the mushroom to completely enclose it.

Transfer the parcels to a greased baking sheet, brush with beaten egg and sprinkle with the sesame seeds. Bake in a preheated oven, 200°C (400°F), Gas Mark 6, for about 25 minutes until golden brown. Serve hot with stir-fried vegetables and soy sauce, if liked.

For French mushroom parcels, drizzle 4 large trimmed field mushrooms with 1 tablespoon olive oil and 2 tablespoons red wine, then top with 2 finely chopped garlic cloves, 2 tablespoons each of chopped basil and chives and 4 slices of goats' cheese cut from a 100 g (3½ oz) piece. Season to taste with salt and pepper, then wrap in pastry as above, brush with beaten egg to glaze and top with a slice of onion. Bake as above.

mixed mushroom bolognese

Serves **4**
Preparation time **20 minutes**,
  plus soaking
Cooking time **1 hour–1 hour
  10 minutes**

25 g (1 oz) **dried wild
  mushrooms**, such as porcini
  and chanterelle
2 tablespoons **olive oil**
1 large **onion**, chopped
1 **celery stick**, finely chopped
1 **carrot**, finely chopped
2 **garlic cloves**, crushed
500 g (1 lb) **mixed
  mushrooms**, trimmed and
  roughly chopped
150 ml (¼ pint) **red wine**
400 g (13 oz) can **chopped
  tomatoes**
1 tablespoon **tomato purée**
1 teaspoon **balsamic vinegar**
2 teaspoons **dried oregano**
300 g (10 oz) **dried spaghetti**
salt and **black pepper**
grated **vegetarian pasta
  cheese**, to serve

Place the dried mushrooms in a bowl and pour over enough hot water to cover. Leave to soak for 20 minutes.

Heat the oil in a large saucepan, add the onion, celery, carrot and garlic and cook over a low heat for 8 minutes, stirring occasionally, until softened. Increase the heat, stir in the mushrooms and cook for 3–4 minutes.

Strain the soaked dried mushrooms through a sieve, reserving the liquid. Add the mushrooms to the pan.

Pour over the wine, bring to the boil and cook until reduced by half. Stir in the reserved soaking liquid, tomatoes, tomato purée, vinegar and oregano, season with salt and pepper and bring to the boil.

Reduce the heat, cover and simmer for 40–50 minutes until the sauce is thick and the mushrooms are tender.

Meanwhile, cook the spaghetti in a large saucepan of lightly salted boiling water for 8–10 minutes, or according to the packet instructions, until al dente. Drain and serve immediately topped with the mushroom mixture, with vegetarian pasta cheese grated over.

For mushroom stroganoff, melt 25 g (1 oz) unsalted butter in a large frying pan, add 500 g (1 lb) mushrooms, trimmed and sliced, and 1 crushed garlic clove and cook for 5–6 minutes until the mushrooms are browned. Stir in 1 teaspoon paprika and 1 tablespoon brandy and cook for 1 minute. Add 300 ml (½ pint) soured cream and simmer for 1 minute, stir in 2 tablespoons chopped parsley and serve with rice.

asparagus & mangetout stir-fry

Serves **4**

Preparation time **10 minutes**

Cooking time **7–10 minutes**

2 tablespoons **vegetable oil**

100 g (3½ oz) **fresh root ginger**, peeled and thinly shredded

2 large **garlic cloves**, thinly sliced

4 **spring onions**, diagonally sliced

250 g (8 oz) **thin asparagus spears**, cut into 3 cm (1¼ inch) lengths

150 g (5 oz) **mangetout**, cut in half diagonally

150 g (5 oz) **bean sprouts**

3 tablespoons **light soy sauce**, plus extra to serve (optional)

Heat a large wok or frying pan until smoking, add the oil and then the ginger and garlic. Stir-fry for 30 seconds. Add the spring onions and stir-fry for 30 seconds, then add the asparagus and stir-fry for a further 3–4 minutes.

Add the mangetout to the pan and stir-fry for 2–3 minutes until the vegetables are still crunchy but beginning to soften.

Stir in the bean sprouts and toss in the hot oil for 1–2 minutes. Pour in the soy sauce, then serve immediately with steamed rice and extra soy sauce, if liked.

For stir-fried vegetable omelettes, follow the recipe above to prepare the stir-fried vegetables and keep warm. For each omelette, beat 3 eggs with 2 tablespoons water and salt and pepper in a bowl. Heat a little vegetable oil in an omelette pan or small frying pan over a medium heat, then swirl in one-quarter of the egg mixture. Fork over the omelette so that it cooks evenly. As soon as it is set on the bottom (but still a little runny in the middle), top with one-quarter of the stir-fried vegetables and cook for a further 30 seconds. Carefully slide the omelette on to a warmed plate, folding it in half as you do so. Keep warm while you make 3 more omelettes in the same way.

savoury bread & butter pudding

Serves **4**
Preparation time **15 minutes**, plus standing
Cooking time **30–35 minutes**

25g (1 oz) **butter**, softened
1 **garlic clove**, crushed
4 thick slices of **stale white bread**
12 **cherry tomatoes**, plus 1 small bunch of **vine cherry tomatoes**
125 g (4 oz) **mature Cheddar cheese**, grated
2 tablespoons chopped **basil**
3 **eggs**
1 teaspoon **smoked paprika**
500 ml (17 fl oz) **milk**
salt and **black pepper**

Mix the butter and garlic together in a small bowl, then grease the bottom of a 1 litre (1¾ pint) shallow ovenproof dish with a little of the butter.

Cut the crusts from the bread, then spread each slice with the remaining butter. Cut each slice in half and arrange half the buttered bread in the bottom of the dish. Scatter over the 12 tomatoes, half the cheese and 1 tablespoon of the basil. Arrange the buttered bread on top and scatter over the remaining basil.

Whisk together the eggs and paprika in a bowl, then whisk in the milk, season with salt and pepper and pour over the bread. Leave to stand for 10 minutes, then scatter over the remaining cheese and top with the bunch of tomatoes. Bake in a preheated oven, 180°C (350°F), Gas Mark 4, for 30–35 minutes until golden and just set. Serve hot with a crisp green salad.

For mushroom & thyme bread pudding, heat 1 tablespoon olive oil in a large frying pan, add 450 g (14½ oz) mixed mushrooms, trimmed and sliced, 1 teaspoon chopped garlic and 2 teaspoons chopped thyme. Cook over a medium heat for 3–4 minutes until softened. Prepare the bread as above, arrange half in the bottom of the buttered dish and top with half the mushroom mixture and ½ x 125 g (4 oz) grated hard goats' cheese. Repeat with the remaining bread and mushrooms. Whisk the eggs and milk as above, omitting the paprika, season with salt and pepper, pour over the bread and mushrooms and leave to stand for 10 minutes. Sprinkle over the remaining cheese and bake as above.

balsamic braised leek & peppers

Serves **4**
Preparation time **5 minutes**
Cooking time **20 minutes**

2 tablespoons **olive oil**
2 **leeks**, trimmed, cleaned and
   cut into 1 cm (½ inch) pieces
1 **orange pepper**, cored,
   deseeded and cut into 1 cm
   (½ inch) chunks
1 **red pepper**, cored,
   deseeded and cut into 1 cm
   (½ inch) chunks
3 tablespoons **balsamic**
   vinegar
handful of **flat leaf parsley**,
   chopped
salt and **black pepper**

Heat the oil in a saucepan, add the leeks and peppers and stir well. Cover and cook very gently for 10 minutes.

Add the vinegar to the pan and cook, uncovered, for a further 10 minutes. The vegetables should be brown from the vinegar and all the liquid should have evaporated.

Season well with salt and pepper, then stir in the chopped parsley just before serving.

For balsamic braised onions, place 500 g (1 lb) baby onions, peeled but left whole, in a saucepan with 3 tablespoons each of balsamic vinegar and olive oil, 40 g (1½ oz) light muscovado sugar, 2 tablespoons sun-dried tomato paste, several thyme sprigs, a handful of sultanas and 300 ml (½ pint) water. Bring to the boil, then reduce the heat and simmer gently, uncovered, for about 40 minutes until the onions are tender and the sauce syrupy. Serve warm or cold.

bean & potato moussaka

Serves **4**

Preparation time **10 minutes,**
plus cooling

Cooking time **55–60 minutes**

750 g (1 ½ lb) medium equal-
sized **potatoes,** washed
1 tablespoon **olive oil**
1 large **onion**, chopped
1 **garlic clove**, crushed
1 large **carrot**, sliced
1 teaspoon **ground cinnamon**
2 teaspoons **dried mixed
herbs**
400 g (13 oz) can **chopped
tomatoes**
400 g (13 oz) can **red kidney
beans**, drained and rinsed
300 ml (½ pint) **vegetable
stock**
salt and **black pepper**

Sauce
50 g (2 oz) **butter**
50 g (2 oz) **plain flour**
600 ml (1 pint) **milk**
75 g (3 oz) **mature Cheddar
cheese**, grated
1 **egg**

Cook the potatoes in a large saucepan of boiling water
for about 10 minutes until just tender. Drain and leave
until cool enough to handle, then remove the skins and
slice into 5 mm (¼ inch) slices.

Heat the oil in a large saucepan, add the onion and
garlic and cook gently for 3–4 minutes until softened.
Add the carrot, cinnamon and herbs, then stir in the
tomatoes, kidney beans and stock. Season to taste
with salt and pepper and bring to the boil, then reduce
the heat and simmer, uncovered, for 15 minutes
until thickened.

Meanwhile, make the sauce. Place the butter, flour and
milk in a saucepan and whisk constantly over a medium
heat until the sauce boils and thickens. Simmer for
2–3 minutes until you have a smooth glossy sauce.
Stir in the cheese and then remove from the heat.
Leave to cool slightly, then beat in the egg.

Place half the bean mixture in the bottom of a deep
ovenproof dish and top with a layer of potatoes. Repeat,
finishing with a layer of potatoes. Pour over the sauce
and bake in a preheated oven, 180°C (350°F), Gas
Mark 4, for 25–30 minutes until golden brown. Leave
to stand for 5 minutes before serving.

For cheesy bean jacket potatoes, scrub 4 x 250 g
(8 oz) King Edward potatoes, then bake in a preheated
oven, 200°C (400°F), Gas Mark 6, for about 1 hour until
cooked through. Meanwhile, follow the recipe above
to prepare the bean filling. Halve the baked potatoes
and spoon over the bean mixture. Grate a little Cheddar
cheese over each and serve immediately.

beetroot chilli with papaya salsa

Serves **4**
Preparation time **15 minutes**
Cooking time **1 hour 35 minutes**

1 tablespoon **sunflower oil**
1 **onion**, chopped
2 **garlic cloves**, finely chopped
500 g (1 lb) **raw beetroot**,
  peeled and cubed
400 g (13 oz) can **red kidney
  beans**, drained and rinsed
1–2 teaspoons **dried chilli flakes**
2 teaspoons **paprika**
1 teaspoon **ground cinnamon**
400 g (13 oz) can **chopped
  tomatoes**
450 ml (¾ pint) **vegetable stock**
2 tablespoons **red wine vinegar**
1 tablespoon **soft dark
  brown sugar**
salt and **black pepper**
brown rice, to serve
soured cream, to serve
mint leaves, chopped, to garnish

Salsa
1 **papaya**, peeled, deseeded
  and diced
½ small **red onion**, finely chopped
1 **tomato**, seeded and diced
small bunch of fresh coriander,
  roughly chopped

Heat the oil in a flameproof casserole, add the onion and cook over a medium heat for 5 minutes until lightly browned. Stir in the garlic, beetroot, kidney beans, chilli flakes and spices, then add the tomatoes, stock, vinegar, sugar and plenty of salt and pepper.

Bring to the boil, then cover and transfer to a preheated oven, 180°C (350°F), Gas Mark 4, for 1½ hours or until the beetroot is tender.

Meanwhile, make the salsa. Mix all the salsa ingredients together in a bowl, then spoon into a serving dish, cover and chill in the refrigerator.

Spoon the brown rice into bowls and top with the chilli and spoonfuls of the salsa. Finish with a dollop of soured cream garnished with the chopped mint leaves.

For beetroot, chilli & orange salad, follow the recipe above to cook the beetroot chilli and leave to cool completely, then stir in the grated rind and juice of 1 orange. Spoon on to lettuce leaves, top with low-fat natural yogurt sprinkled with mint leaves and garnish with orange segments.

soups
& stews

singapore noodle soup

Serves **4**
Preparation time **5 minutes**,
  plus standing
Cooking time **5 minutes**

200 g (7 oz) **dried flat
  rice noodles**
1 tablespoon **Singapore
  noodle paste**
100 g (3½ oz) **green beans**
1 **carrot**, cut into thin strips
400 ml (13 fl oz) can **reduced-
  fat coconut milk**
750 ml (1¼ pints) **hot
  vegetable stock**
100 g (3½ oz) **bean sprouts**
225 g (7½ oz) can **bamboo
  shoots**, drained
2 tablespoons chopped **fresh
  coriander**
2 tablespoons **lime juice**

To serve
4 **spring onions**, thinly sliced
1 small **red chilli**, thinly sliced
  (optional)

Place the noodles in a large heatproof bowl, pour over boiling water to cover and leave to stand for 5 minutes or until just tender.

Meanwhile, place the Singapore noodle paste in a large saucepan, add the beans and carrot and stir together thoroughly until the vegetables are coated in the spice mix. Cook, stirring, over a medium heat for 1–2 minutes.

Stir the coconut milk and hot stock into the pan, then add the bean sprouts and bamboo shoots and simmer for 3 minutes. Stir in the coriander and the lime juice.

Drain the noodles, divide between 4 warmed large deep bowls and ladle over the soup.

Top with the spring onions and chilli, if using, and serve immediately with lime wedges.

For miso noodle & mushroom soup, dissolve 4 x 10g (⅓ oz) sachets miso soup mix in 1 litre (1¾ pints) boiling water in a saucepan. Add 2 teaspoons peeled and chopped fresh root ginger and 150 g (5 oz) each Tenderstem broccoli tips and shiitake mushrooms, trimmed and sliced. Cover and simmer for 4–5 minutes until the vegetables are tender. Stir in 125 g (4 oz) dried rice noodles. Cook for a further 2–3 minutes or until the noodles are just tender. Serve immediately in warmed bowls.

apple & leek soup

Serves **4**
Preparation time **10 minutes**
Cooking time **25 minutes**

25 g (1 oz) **butter**
1 tablespoon **sunflower oil**
450 g (1 lb) **leeks**, trimmed,
  cleaned and sliced
2 **potatoes**, peeled and diced
2 **dessert apples**, peeled,
  cored and diced
150 ml (¼ pint) **dry cider**
900 ml (1½ pints) **vegetable
  stock**
salt and **black pepper**
grated **Gruyère cheese**,
  to serve

Melt the butter with the oil in a large saucepan over a medium heat, add the leeks and cook for 5 minutes until starting to soften.

Stir the potatoes and apples into the pan, cover and cook for a further 5 minutes.

Add the cider and cook, uncovered, until reduced by half. Stir in the stock, cover and simmer for 15 minutes until the potatoes are tender.

Serve topped with grated Gruyère cheese.

For leek & white bean soup, heat 2 tablespoons olive oil in a large saucepan, add 450 g (1 lb) leeks, trimmed, cleaned and sliced, and cook for 5 minutes until softened. Stir in 300 g (10 oz) potatoes, peeled and diced, a 400 g (13 oz) can cannellini beans, drained and rinsed, and 1 litre (1¾ pints) hot vegetable stock. Bring to the boil, then cover and simmer for 20 minutes until the vegetables are tender. Stir in 2 tablespoons chopped parsley and serve immediately with freshly ground black pepper.

summer vegetable pistou

Serves **4**
Preparation time **15 minutes**
Cooking time **30 minutes**

2 tablespoons **olive oil**
1 **onion**, chopped
2 **garlic cloves**, crushed
600 ml (1 pint) **vegetable stock**
250 g (8 oz) **baby new potatoes**, scrubbed and halved
250 g (8 oz) **baby carrots**
200 g (7 oz) **baby courgettes**, halved lengthways
4 **tomatoes**, skinned and chopped
200 g (7 oz) **fresh peas**
salt and **black pepper**
4 tablespoons **fresh pesto sauce** (see right for homemade), to serve

Heat the oil in a large saucepan, add the onion and garlic and cook for 2–3 minutes until softened.

Pour over the stock, bring to the boil and add the potatoes. Cover, reduce the heat and simmer for 10 minutes.

Add the carrots, courgettes and tomatoes, re-cover and simmer for a further 10 minutes. Stir in the peas and cook for 4–5 minutes or until all the vegetables are tender. Season to taste with salt and pepper.

Ladle the soup into large warmed bowls and serve each topped with a tablespoon of pesto, along with crusty bread rolls, if liked.

For homemade fresh pesto sauce, place 2 crushed garlic cloves in a food processor with 75 g (3 oz) basil leaves and 3 tablespoons pine nuts and blitz until the mixture forms a paste. Add 3 tablespoons grated vegetarian pasta cheese and then, with the motor running, gradually pour in 100 ml (3½ fl oz) olive oil through the food tube in a thin steady stream until smooth. Season to taste with salt and pepper.

curried parsnip soup

Serves **4**
Preparation time **15 minutes**
Cooking time **30–35 minutes**

25 g (1 oz) **butter**
1 tablespoon **sunflower oil**
1 **onion**, chopped
2 **garlic cloves**, crushed
2.5cm (1 inch) piece of **fresh root ginger**, peeled and chopped
1 tablespoon **medium curry powder**
1 teaspoon **cumin seeds**
750 g (1½ lb) **parsnips**, peeled and chopped
1 litre (1¾ pints) **vegetable stock**
salt and **black pepper**

To serve
natural yogurt
2 tablespoons chopped **fresh coriander**
naan bread

Melt the butter with the oil in a large saucepan, add the onion, garlic and ginger and cook over a medium heat for 4–5 minutes until softened.

Stir in the curry powder and cumin seeds and cook, stirring, for 2 minutes, then stir in the parsnips, making sure that they are well coated in the spice mixture.

Pour over the stock and bring to the boil, then cover and simmer for 20–25 minutes until the parsnips are tender. Season to taste with salt and pepper.

Blend the soup with a stick blender until smooth, or transfer to a food processor or blender, in batches, to blend. Reheat gently if necessary.

Serve in cups with dollops of natural yogurt, garnished with the coriander and with warmed naan bread.

For caramelized parsnip & honey soup, melt 25 g (1 oz) unsalted butter in a flameproof roasting tin on the hob, add the peeled and chopped parsnips and 2 thyme sprigs and turn to coat in the butter. Roast in a preheated oven, 200°C (400° F), Gas Mark 6, for 30–35 minutes, stirring once, until golden brown. Stir in 2 tablespoons clear honey and roast for a further 10 minutes until the parsnips have caramelized. Transfer to a saucepan, stir in 1 litre (1¾ pints) vegetable stock and bring to the boil on the hob, then simmer for 10 minutes. Transfer to a food processor or blender, in batches, and blend until smooth. Return to the pan, season to taste with salt and pepper and stir in 300 ml (½ pint) boiling water, then bring back to the boil. Stir in 4 tablespoons double cream and gently heat through. Serve in bowls with crusty bread.

beetroot & horseradish soup

Serves **4**
Preparation time **15 minutes**
Cooking time **30–35 minutes**

1 tablespoon **sunflower oil**
1 **red onion**, chopped
1 **celery stick**, chopped
1 teaspoon chopped **thyme**
500 g (1 lb) **raw beetroot**,
   peeled and cut into small
   chunks
1 tablespoon **red wine**
   vinegar
900 ml (1½ pints) hot
   vegetable stock
2 tablespoons **creamed**
   horseradish sauce, plus
   2 teaspoons
3 tablespoons **soured cream**
   or **crème fraîche**
salt and **black pepper**
chopped **chives**, to garnish
crusty bread, to serve

Heat the oil in a large saucepan, add the onion, celery and thyme and cook gently for 3–4 minutes. Add the beetroot and vinegar and cook for 2 minutes.

Pour over the stock, cover and simmer for about 25 minutes until the beetroot is tender. Season to taste with salt and pepper and stir in the horseradish sauce.

Blend the soup with a stick blender until smooth, or transfer to a food processor or blender, in batches, to blend. Reheat gently if necessary.

Mix the soured cream or crème fraîche with the remaining horseradish sauce. Spoon on top of the soup and garnish with chopped chives. Serve with crusty bread.

For beetroot & caraway soup, heat 1 tablespoon sunflower oil in a large saucepan, add 1 chopped onion and 1 crushed garlic clove and cook gently for 3–4 minutes until softened. Stir in 1 teaspoon caraway seeds, 500 g (1 lb) raw beetroot, peeled and diced, 1 medium potato, peeled and diced, 1 tablespoon cider vinegar and 900 ml (1½ pints) vegetable stock. Cover and simmer for 30 minutes until the beetroot and potato are tender. Season to taste with salt and pepper, then blend with a stick blender until smooth, or transfer to a food processor or blender, in batches, to blend. Reheat gently if necessary. Serve topped with a spoonful of Greek yogurt and a sprinkling of caraway seeds.

potato & smoked garlic soup

Serves **4**
Preparation time **10–15
minutes**
Cooking time **30–35 minutes**

50 g (2 oz) **unsalted butter**
1 large **onion**, sliced
2 **smoked garlic cloves**,
  crushed
750 g (1½ lb) **floury
  potatoes**, peeled and cut
  into small cubes
1 litre (1¾ pints) **vegetable
  stock**
½ teaspoon **smoked sea salt**
125 ml (4 fl oz) **milk**
4 tablespoons **fresh herbs**,
  such as parsley, thyme and
  chives, plus extra snipped
  chives to garnish
black pepper
Greek yogurt, to serve

Melt the butter in a large saucepan, add the onion
and smoked garlic and cook over a medium heat for
3–4 minutes until softened. Stir in the potatoes, cover
and cook for 5 minutes.

Add the stock and season with the smoked sea salt and
pepper. Bring to the boil, then reduce the heat, cover
and simmer for 30 minutes until the potatoes
are tender.

Transfer to a food processor or blender, in batches, and
blend until smooth. Return to the pan, stir in the milk
and herbs and reheat gently.

Serve in warmed bowls with a spoonful of Greek
yogurt, garnished with chives and freshly ground
black pepper.

For smoked sweet potato soup, cook the onion and
garlic as above, then add 1 tablespoon smoked paprika
and cook, stirring, for 1 minute. Stir in 300 g (10 oz)
potato and 450 g (1 lb) sweet potato, both peeled and
cut into small cubes, and cook for 5 minutes. Add the
stock as above and bring to the boil, then cover and
simmer for 30 minutes until the potato is tender. Blend
as above until smooth, then serve with a spoonful of
Greek yogurt, garnished with a sprinkling of smoked
paprika and freshly snipped chives.

butter bean & vegetable soup

Serves **4**
Preparation time **10 minutes**
Cooking time **25 minutes**

1 tablespoon **olive oil**
2 teaspoons **smoked paprika**
1 **celery stick**, sliced
2 **carrots**, sliced
1 **leek**, trimmed, cleaned
   and sliced
600 ml (1 pint) **vegetable
   stock**
400 g (13 oz) can **chopped
   tomatoes**
400 g (13 oz) can **butter
   beans**, drained and rinsed
2 teaspoons chopped
   rosemary
salt and **black pepper**
50 g (2 oz) **vegetarian pasta
   cheese**, grated, to serve

Heat the oil in a large saucepan, add the paprika, celery, carrots and leek and cook over a medium heat for 3–4 minutes until the vegetables are slightly softened.

Pour over the stock and tomatoes and add the butter beans and rosemary. Season to taste with salt and pepper and bring to the boil, then cover and simmer for 15 minutes or until the vegetables are just tender.

Ladle into warmed bowls and sprinkle with the cheese and freshly ground black pepper.

For minestrone soup, soften the vegetables in the oil as above, then add the stock, tomatoes and rosemary with a 400 g (13 oz) can borlotti beans, drained and rinsed, in place of the butter beans, and simmer for 10 minutes. Add 75 g (3 oz) dried spaghetti, broken into small pieces, and 125 g (4 oz) shredded green cabbage and simmer for a further 8 minutes until the pasta is tender, stirring occasionally. Serve in warmed bowls, sprinkled with the grated vegetarian pasta cheese as above.

lemon grass & sweet potato curry

Serves **4**
Preparation time **15 minutes**
Cooking time **20 minutes**

2 **lemon grass stalks**
400 ml (13 fl oz) can **coconut milk**
150 ml (¼ pint) **vegetable stock**
1 **garlic clove**, crushed
2.5 cm (1 inch) piece of **fresh root ginger**, peeled and finely chopped
1 **red chilli**, deseeded and chopped
2 teaspoons **palm sugar** or **soft light brown sugar**
6 **kaffir lime leaves**
450 g (14½ oz) **sweet potatoes**, peeled and chopped
1 **red pepper,** cored, deseeded and chopped
200 g (7 oz) **baby spinach leaves**
2 tablespoons **lime juice**
handful of **fresh coriander** or **Thai basil leaves**
steamed jasmine rice, to serve

Remove the tough outer stems from the lemon grass, then cut into 2.5 cm (1 inch) pieces.

Place the coconut milk, stock, garlic, ginger, chilli, lemon grass, sugar and lime leaves in a large saucepan and bring to the boil. Add the sweet potatoes, cover and simmer for 10 minutes.

Add the red pepper to the pan and cook for a further 5 minutes.

Stir in the spinach and lime juice, re-cover and cook for 2–3 minutes until the spinach has wilted, then stir in the coriander or Thai basil. Serve immediately with steamed jasmine rice.

For Thai massaman vegetable curry, cut 350 g (11½ oz) scrubbed new potatoes into small pieces and cook in a saucepan of boiling water for 4 minutes until just tender, then drain. Meanwhile, heat 1 tablespoon sunflower oil in a separate saucepan, add 400 g (13 oz) mixed chopped vegetables, such as carrots, green beans and courgettes, and 3 tablespoons vegetarian Thai massaman curry paste and cook, stirring frequently, for 3–4 minutes. Pour over a 400 ml (14 fl oz) can coconut milk, stir in 2 kaffir lime leaves and bring to the boil. Add the potatoes, then reduce the heat, cover and simmer for 10 minutes until the vegetables are tender. Serve garnished with a large handful of unsalted peanuts.

quick vegetable mole

Serves **4**
Preparation time **10 minutes**
Cooking time **30–35 minutes**

1 tablespoon **sunflower oil**
1 large **onion**, chopped
1 **garlic clove**, crushed
400 g (13 oz) **sweet potatoes**, peeled and cut into small chunks
1 large **red pepper**, cored, deseeded and chopped
1 tablespoon **chilli powder**
2 x 400 g (13 oz) cans **chopped tomatoes**
150 ml (¼ pint) **vegetable stock**
400 g (13 oz) can **red kidney beans**, drained and rinsed
400 g (13 oz) can **black beans**, drained and rinsed
15 g (½ oz) **plain dark chocolate**, grated
2 tablespoons chopped **fresh coriander**
salt and **black pepper**
soured cream, to serve

Heat the oil in a large saucepan, add the onion and garlic and cook over a medium heat for 2–3 minutes until softened. Add the sweet potatoes and red pepper and cook for 2 minutes.

Stir in the chilli powder, tomatoes, stock and all the beans and bring to the boil. Reduce the heat, cover and simmer gently for 20–25 minutes until the vegetables are tender. Season to taste with salt and pepper.

Add the chocolate and coriander and cook for a further 2–3 minutes. Serve with long-grain rice topped with spoonfuls of soured cream.

For Mexican bean soup, heat 1 tablespoon sunflower oil in a frying pan, add 1 chopped onion, 1 chopped celery stick, 2 diced carrots and 1 cored, deseeded and chopped red pepper and cook over a medium heat for 5–6 minutes until softened. Stir in 1 tablespoon chilli powder, 400 g (13 oz) can chopped tomatoes, a 400 g (13 oz) can each of red kidney beans and black beans, drained and rinsed, and 600 ml (1 pint) hot vegetable stock. Simmer for 10 minutes. Stir in 15 g (½ oz) grated plain dark chocolate and serve in bowls, garnished with chopped spring onions, chopped fresh coriander and a spoonful of soured cream.

mango & coconut curry

Serves **4**

Preparation time **20 minutes**

Cooking time about **20 minutes**

300 g (10 oz) **fresh coconut,** grated

3–4 fresh **green chillies**, roughly chopped

1 tablespoon **cumin seeds**

500 ml (17 fl oz) **water**

3 firm ripe **mangoes**, peeled, stoned and cubed

1 teaspoon **ground turmeric**

1 teaspoon **chilli powder**

300 ml (½ pint) **fat-free natural yogurt**, lightly whisked

1 tablespoon **groundnut oil**

2 teaspoons **black mustard seeds**

3–4 hot **dried red chillies**

10–12 **curry leaves**

Place the coconut, fresh chillies and cumin seeds in a food processor with half the measurement water and blend to a fine paste.

Combine the mangoes with the turmeric, chilli powder and the remaining measurement water in a heavy saucepan. Bring to the boil, add the coconut paste and stir to mix well. Cover and simmer over a medium heat for 10–12 minutes, stirring occasionally, until the mixture becomes fairly thick.

Add the yogurt and heat gently, stirring, until just warmed through. Do not let the mixture come to the boil or it will curdle. Remove from the heat and keep warm.

Heat the oil in a small frying pan over a medium-high heat. Add the mustard seeds and as soon as they begin to pop (after a few seconds), add the dried chillies and curry leaves. Stir-fry for a few seconds until the chillies darken. Stir into the mango curry and serve immediately.

chickpea & aubergine tagine

Serves **4**
Preparation time **10 minutes**
Cooking time **45 minutes**

1 tablespoon **sunflower oil**
1 large **onion**, sliced
2 **garlic cloves**, crushed
1 teaspoon **ground cumin**
1 teaspoon **ground cinnamon**
1 teaspoon **ground turmeric**
1 teaspoon **ground paprika**
2 **aubergines**, chopped into
   3.5 cm (1½ inch) chunks
2 **carrots**, sliced
125 g (4 oz) **soft dried
   pitted dates**
400 g (13 oz) can **chopped
   tomatoes**
400 g (13 oz) can **chickpeas**,
   drained and rinsed
600 ml (1 pint) **vegetable
   stock**
4 slices of **preserved lemon**
2 tablespoons chopped **flat
   leaf parsley**
salt and **black pepper**
couscous, to serve

Heat the oil in a large saucepan, add the onion and garlic and cook over a medium heat for 4–5 minutes until softened. Stir in all the spices and cook, stirring, for 1 minute.

Add the aubergines and cook for about 5 minutes until starting to soften. Stir in all the remaining ingredients, except the parsley, and season to taste with salt and pepper.

Bring to the boil, then reduce the heat, cover and simmer for 30 minutes, stirring occasionally.

Stir in the parsley, then serve in warmed deep bowls with couscous.

For chickpea, apricot & almond tagine, cook the onion and garlic as above, then stir in 2 teaspoons harissa paste and 1 teaspoon ground cinnamon and cook, stirring, for 1 minute. Add the aubergines and cook as above, then add the remaining ingredients, using 125 g (4 oz) ready-to-eat dried apricots in place of the dates. Cook as above, then stir in the parsley, scatter with 50 g (2 oz) toasted blanched almonds and serve with couscous.

spinach & tomato dhal

Serves **4**
Preparation time **10 minutes**
Cooking time **1 hour**

250 g (8 oz) **dried red split
  lentils**, rinsed and drained
½ teaspoon **ground turmeric**
2 **green chillies**, deseeded
  and chopped
2 teaspoons peeled and
  grated **fresh root ginger**
1 litre (1¾ pints) **water**
400 g (13 oz) can **chopped
  tomatoes**
250 g (8 oz) **baby spinach
  leaves**
salt

Spiced oil
1 tablespoon **sunflower oil**
1 **shallot**, thinly sliced
12 **curry leaves**
1 teaspoon **black mustard
  seeds**
1 teaspoon **cumin seeds**
1 **dried red chilli**, broken into
  small pieces

Place the lentils in a large saucepan with the turmeric,
chillies, ginger and measurement water. Bring to the
boil, then reduce the heat and simmer, uncovered,
for 40 minutes or until the lentils have broken down
and the mixture has thickened.

Add the tomatoes and cook for a further 10 minutes
or until thickened. Stir in the spinach and cook for
2–3 minutes until wilted.

Prepare the spiced oil. Heat the oil in a small frying
pan, add the shallot and cook over a medium-high heat,
stirring, for 2–3 minutes until golden brown. Add all the
remaining ingredients and cook, stirring constantly, for
1–2 minutes until the seeds start to pop.

Tip the spiced oil into the dhal, stir well and season
to taste with salt. Serve with naan bread or steamed
basmati rice, if liked.

For coconut & spinach dhal, follow the recipe above
to cook the lentils with the turmeric, chillies, ginger
and measurement water for 40 minutes. Continue as
above, using 200 ml (7 fl oz) canned coconut milk
and 4 chopped fresh tomatoes in place of the canned
chopped tomatoes. Serve the dhal with naan bread.

salads
& sides

crisp parsnip cakes

Serves **4**
Preparation time **10 minutes**
Cooking time **20–25 minutes**

750 g (1 ½ lb) **parsnips**,
   peeled and chopped
50 g (2 oz) **butter**
1 **garlic clove**, crushed
1 tablespoon chopped **thyme**
2 tablespoons **sunflower oil**
salt and **black pepper**

Cook the parsnips in a large saucepan of lightly salted boiling water for 10 minutes until tender.

Meanwhile, melt the butter in a small frying pan, add the garlic and thyme and cook gently, stirring, for 2 minutes.

Drain the parsnips, return to the pan and mash thoroughly. Mash in the buttery garlic mixture and season well with salt and pepper. Leave until cool enough to handle.

Shape the parsnip mixture into 8 patties with lightly floured hands.

Heat 1 tablespoon of the oil in a large frying pan, add 4 of the patties and cook for 3–4 minutes on each side until golden brown. Transfer the patties to a baking sheet and keep warm in a low oven while you repeat with the remaining oil and patties. Serve warm.

For curried parsnip patties, cook the parsnips as above. Melt 50 g (2 oz) butter in a frying pan, add 1 crushed garlic clove and 1 tablespoon medium curry powder and cook, stirring, for 2 minutes. Drain the parsnips, return to the pan and mash thoroughly. Beat in the spiced butter mixture with 2 tablespoons chopped fresh coriander. Shape into patties and fry as above.

cannellini & green bean salad

Serves **4**
Preparation time **15 minutes**
Cooking time **12–15 minutes**

300 g (10 oz) small **new potatoes**, scrubbed and halved
200 g (7 oz) **fine green beans**, topped and tailed and halved
400 g (13 oz) can **cannellini beans**, drained and rinsed
75 g (3 oz) **pitted black olives**, sliced
½ small **red onion**, thinly sliced
4 tablespoons **extra virgin olive oil**
grated rind and juice of **1 large lemon**
pinch of **caster sugar**
2 tablespoons chopped **mint**
2 tablespoons chopped **flat leaf parsley**
salt and **black pepper**

Cook the potatoes in a large saucepan of boiling water for 12–15 minutes until tender, adding the green beans for the last 3 minutes. Drain and refresh under cold running water.

Place the cannellini beans, olives and onion in a large bowl and stir in the potatoes and green beans.

Whisk together the oil, lemon rind and juice, sugar and salt and pepper in a jug, then stir in the chopped herbs. Pour over the bean and potato mixture and toss well before serving.

For white bean & tomato salad, place 2 x 400 g (13 oz) cans cannellini or butter beans, drained and rinsed, in a bowl and stir in 250 g (8 oz) halved vine cherry tomatoes and 2 tablespoons chopped flat leaf parsley. Whisk together 4 tablespoons extra virgin olive oil, the juice of 1 lemon, 1 teaspoon Dijon mustard and 1 crushed garlic clove in a jug. Season to taste with salt and pepper. Pour over the bean and tomato mixture and gently toss together. Serve with toasted ciabatta, if liked.

herb-roasted new potatoes

Serves **6**
Preparation time **10 minutes**
Cooking time **45–50 minutes**

2 tablespoons **olive oil**
1 kg (2 lb) **new potatoes**,
  scrubbed
4 **garlic cloves**, peeled but
  left whole
2 **rosemary sprigs**
2 **thyme sprigs**
1 **sage sprig**
sea salt and **black pepper**

Put the oil into a roasting tin and place in a preheated oven, 200°C (400°F), Gas Mark 6, for 5 minutes until hot.

Add the potatoes, garlic cloves and herb sprigs, season well with sea salt and pepper and turn to coat in the oil.

Return to the oven and roast for 40–45 minutes, turning occasionally, until the potatoes are crisp and tender. Serve hot.

For crushed new potatoes with spring onions & mustard, cook 1 kg (2 lb) scrubbed new potatoes in a large saucepan of lightly salted boiling water for 15 minutes or until tender. Drain well, return to the pan and add 2 tablespoons olive oil and 1 tablespoon wholegrain mustard. Crush with a fork until the potatoes are broken up but not mashed, then stir in 4 chopped spring onions. Season to taste with salt and pepper and serve immediately.

roast tomato & mozzarella salad

Serves **4**
Preparation time **10 minutes**,
  plus cooling
Cooking time **20 minutes**

250 g (8 oz) **baby plum** or
  cherry tomatoes, halved
1 tablespoon **olive oil**
150 g (5 oz) **mini mozzarella
  balls**, drained
25 g (1 oz) **pine nuts**, toasted
sea salt and **black pepper**

Dressing
25 g (1 oz) **rocket leaves**
12 **basil leaves**
4 tablespoons **extra virgin
  olive oil**
1 teaspoon **red wine vinegar**

Place the tomatoes, cut-side up, in a small roasting tin. Drizzle over the olive oil and season with a little sea salt and pepper. Roast in a preheated oven, 200°C (400°F), Gas Mark 6, for 20 minutes until wilted and softened. Remove from the oven and leave to cool.

Make the dressing. Place the rocket and basil leaves, 2 tablespoons of the extra virgin olive oil and the vinegar in a small bowl. Blend with a stick blender to a purée, or transfer to a mini food processor to blend. Stir in the remaining oil and season to taste with salt and pepper.

Arrange the roasted tomatoes on a platter, then tear the mozzarella balls in half and arrange among the tomatoes. Drizzle over the dressing and scatter over the pine nuts. Serve immediately with ciabatta.

For basil dressing, to serve as an alternative dressing for the salad, use 20 g (¾ oz) basil leaves in place of the rocket and basil and follow the recipe above to prepare the dressing. Serve the salad with a handful of rocket leaves.

ginger, coconut & lime leaf rice

Serves **4**
Preparation time **10 minutes**,
   plus standing
Cooking time **15 minutes**

250 g (8 oz) **jasmine rice**
2 teaspoons peeled and
   chopped **fresh root ginger**
300 ml (½ pint) **coconut milk**
6 **kaffir lime leaves**, bashed
1 **lemon grass stalk**, halved
   and bruised
1 teaspoon **salt**
250 ml (8 fl oz) **water**

Place the rice in a sieve and rinse in cold water until the water runs clear. Drain and shake well.

Combine the rice with all the remaining ingredients in a saucepan with a tight-fitting lid. Bring to the boil, cover with the lid and cook over a low heat for 10 minutes.

Remove from the heat and leave to stand, covered and without stirring, for 10 minutes. Fluff up with a fork before serving.

For cardamom & lemon rice, rinse and drain 250 g (8 oz) basmati rice as above. Heat 1 tablespoon sunflower oil in a large saucepan with a tight-fitting lid, add 1 chopped onion and cook gently for 2–3 minutes until softened. Stir in 6 crushed cardamom pods and the rice and stir-fry for 2–3 minutes, then pour over 475 ml (16 fl oz) boiling water. Season with salt and stir well, then cover with the lid and cook over a low heat for 10 minutes. Remove from the heat and stir in the juice of 2 lemons. Leave to stand, covered and without stirring, for 10 minutes. Fluff up with a fork before serving.

apple, blue cheese & nut salad

Serves **4**
Preparation time **15 minutes**,
  plus cooling
Cooking time **10–12 minutes**

15 g (½ oz) **unsalted butter**
2 tablespoons **caster sugar**
2 **red dessert apples**, cored
  and cut into thin wedges
75 g (3 oz) **walnut pieces**
½ small **red cabbage**, thinly
  sliced
2 **celery sticks**, chopped
150 g (5 oz) v**egetarian blue
  cheese**, such as dolcelatte,
  crumbled

Dressing
2 tablespoons **walnut oil**
2 tablespoons **olive oil**
2 tablespoons **balsamic
  vinegar**
salt and **black pepper**

Melt the butter in a frying pan, add the sugar and stir over a low heat until the sugar has dissolved.

Add the apples to the pan and cook for 3–4 minutes on each side until they start to caramelize, then stir in the walnuts and cook for 1 minute. Remove from the heat and leave to cool.

Place the red cabbage and celery in a bowl, then add the cooled apple and walnut mixture.

Make the dressing. Place the oils and vinegar in a screw-top jar with salt and pepper to taste, add the lid and shake well.

Drizzle the dressing over the ingredients in the bowl and toss together. Serve immediately, scattered with the blue cheese.

For pear, spinach & Stilton salad, melt the butter and heat the sugar until dissolved as above. Add 2 cored and thinly sliced firm but ripe pears in place of the apples and cook until caramelized, then stir in the walnuts as above. Place 200 g (7 oz) baby spinach leaves in a bowl, instead of the red cabbage and celery, and add the pear and walnut mixture. Prepare the dressing as above, add to the bowl and gently coat the salad ingredients in the dressing. Scatter with 150 g (5 oz) crumbled Stilton and serve immediately.

sweet potato & garlic mash

Serves **4**
Preparation time **10 minutes**
Cooking time **15–20 minutes**

1 kg (2 lb) **sweet potatoes**,
   peeled and cut into 2.5 cm
   (1 inch) pieces
4–6 **smoked garlic cloves**,
   peeled but left whole
25 g (1 oz) **salted butter**
2 tablespoons **milk**
2 tablespoons chopped **flat
   leaf parsley**
salt and **black pepper**

Place the sweet potatoes and smoked garlic cloves in a large saucepan, cover with cold water and bring to the boil. Reduce the heat and simmer for 10–12 minutes until tender, then drain well.

Return the sweet potatoes and garlic to the pan and mash until smooth.

Set the pan over a low heat, then push the mash to one side, add the butter to the base of the pan and leave to melt. Pour the milk on to the butter and heat for 1–2 minutes, then beat into the mash.

Stir in the parsley, season to taste with salt and pepper and serve.

For sweet potato, cheese & mustard mash, cook the potatoes as above, omitting the smoked garlic, then beat in the butter and milk with 2 tablespoons wholegrain mustard and 125 g (4 oz) grated mature Cheddar cheese. Stir in 2 tablespoons chopped chives, season to taste with salt and pepper and serve.

thai rice salad

Serves **4**
Preparation time **20 minutes**

250 g (8 oz) freshly cooked
mixed **long-grain** and **wild
rice**, cooled
2 **carrots**, thinly sliced
½ **cucumber,** halved,
deseeded and thinly sliced
1 **red pepper**, cored,
deseeded and thinly sliced
75 g (3 oz) **bean sprouts**
4 **spring onions**, thinly sliced
4 tablespoons chopped
fresh coriander
50 g (2 oz) **roasted unsalted
peanuts**, roughly chopped
lime wedges, to serve

Dressing
4 tablespoons **sweet chilli
sauce**
grated rind and juice of
2 **limes**
2 teaspoons **light soy sauce**

Place the cooked rice, carrots, cucumber, red pepper,
bean sprouts, spring onions and coriander in a large
bowl and mix together thoroughly.

Make the dressing. Whisk the dressing ingredients
together in a small bowl, then pour over the salad and
toss to coat.

Scatter the salad with the peanuts and serve
immediately with lime wedges.

For Vietnamese rice noodle salad, place 150 g
(5 oz) dried rice noodles in a large heatproof bowl and
pour over boiling water to cover. Leave to stand for
3 minutes, then drain and refresh under cold running
water. Leave to drain. Place the carrots, cucumber, red
pepper, bean sprouts, spring onions and peanuts as
above in a large bowl and add the drained noodles.
Whisk together 4 tablespoons lime juice, 3 tablespoons
sweet chilli sauce, 2 tablespoons rice wine vinegar
and 1 tablespoon light soy sauce in a small bowl,
pour over the noodle mixture and toss to coat. Stir
in 4 tablespoons each of chopped mint and fresh
coriander. Serve in bowls, garnished with mint leaves.

mustard griddled potatoes

Serves **2**
Preparation time **10 minutes**,
  plus standing
Cooking time **25 minutes**

500 g (1 lb) **waxy potatoes**,
  scrubbed and cut into 1 cm
  (½ inch) thick slices
2 tablespoons **olive oil**
½ teaspoon **sea salt**
2 teaspoons **wholegrain
  mustard**
1 tablespoon chopped
  tarragon
sea salt and **black pepper**

Cook the potatoes in a saucepan of lightly salted boiling water for 10 minutes. Drain well and leave to dry for a few minutes.

Place 1 tablespoon of the oil in a large bowl with the sea salt and a generous grinding of pepper, add the potatoes and turn gently to coat in the oil.

Heat a large griddle pan over a medium heat, and when hot, add the potatoes in a single layer. Cook for 3 minutes on each side until golden. Remove and keep warm while you cook any remaining potatoes.

Whisk the remaining oil, mustard and tarragon together in a small bowl. Place the potatoes in a shallow bowl and pour over the dressing. Serve immediately.

For paprika griddled potatoes, cook the potatoes in boiling water, then drain well and leave to dry as above. Mix 2 tablespoons olive oil with 1–2 teaspoons smoked paprika and a little salt and pepper in a large bowl. Add the potatoes and stir gently to coat in the paprika oil. Cook in a large griddle pan as above and serve sprinkled with chopped flat leaf parsley.

breads &
baking

cheat's mediterranean focaccia

Serves **8**
Preparation time **15 minutes**
Cooking time **15 minutes**

olive oil, for brushing
450 g (14½ oz) **plain flour**
1 teaspoon **bicarbonate
 of soda**
1 teaspoon **salt**
1 tablespoon chopped
 rosemary, plus 10 small
 sprigs
100 g (3½ oz) **sun-dried
 tomatoes**, chopped
400 ml (14 fl oz) **buttermilk**
10 pitted **black olives**
1 teaspoon **sea salt**

Brush a 23 cm x 32 cm (9 inch x 12½ inch) Swiss roll tin generously with oil.

Sift the flour, bicarbonate of soda and salt into a large bowl. Stir in the chopped rosemary and sun-dried tomatoes. Make a well in the centre, add the buttermilk to the well and gradually stir into the flour. Bring the mixture together with your hands to form a soft, slightly sticky dough.

Tip the dough out on to a lightly floured surface and lightly knead for 1 minute, then quickly roll into a rectangular shape to fit the prepared tin. Press the dough gently into the tin, then brush with oil. Using your finger, make small dimples in the top of the bread. Scatter over the black olives, rosemary sprigs and sea salt.

Bake in a preheated oven, 220°C (425°F), Gas Mark 7, for 15 minutes until brown and crisp. Brush with a little more olive oil and serve warm.

For cheese & onion focaccia, prepare the bread as above, omitting the sun-dried tomatoes and rosemary. Scatter 75 g (3 oz) finely sliced red onion and 25 g (1 oz) freshly grated vegetarian cheese over the top and bake as above.

spinach, feta & egg tarts

Makes **4**
Preparation time **15 minutes**
Cooking time **16–18 minutes**

250 g (8 oz) **frozen leaf
  spinach**, defrosted
125 g (4 oz) **feta cheese**,
  diced
2 tablespoons **mascarpone
  cheese**
pinch of freshly grated **nutmeg**
4 sheets of **filo pastry**,
  defrosted if frozen
50 g (2 oz) **butter**, melted
4 **eggs**
salt and **black pepper**

Drain the spinach and squeeze out all the excess water, then chop finely. Place in a bowl and mix in the feta, mascarpone, nutmeg and salt and pepper to taste.

Lay the sheets of filo pastry on top of one another in a pile, brushing each with a little melted butter. Cut out 4 x 15 cm (6 inch) rounds using a saucer as a template.

Divide the spinach mixture between the pastry rounds, spreading the filling out but leaving a 2.5 cm (1 inch) border. Gather the edges up and over the filling to form a rim. Make a shallow well in the spinach mixture.

Transfer the tarts to a baking sheet and bake in a preheated oven, 200°C (400°F), Gas Mark 6, for 8 minutes. Remove from the oven and carefully crack an egg into each hollow. Bake for a further 8–10 minutes until the eggs are set.

For spinach & goats' cheese parcels, prepare the spinach as above, then mix with 125 g (4 oz) soft goats' cheese, 2 tablespoons mascarpone cheese, a pinch of ground cumin and salt and pepper to taste. Cut out the filo pastry rounds as above and divide the spinach mixture between them, but place it on one half of each round. Carefully fold the pastry over the filling and turn the pastry edges over to seal. Bake in the oven as above and serve with lemon wedges for squeezing over and Greek yogurt.

sweet potato & onion seed rolls

Makes **8**
Preparation time **30 minutes**,
  plus standing and rising
Cooking time **30–35 minutes**

350 g (11½ oz) **sweet
  potatoes**, peeled
  and chopped
1 tablespoon **olive oil**
1 teaspoon **fast-action
  dried yeast**
300 g (10 oz) **strong
  white flour**
½ teaspoon **salt**
½ teaspoon **ground black
  pepper**
1 teaspoon **black onion
  seeds**

Cook the sweet potatoes in a saucepan of boiling water for about 15 minutes until tender. Drain, reserving 5 tablespoons of the cooking water. Return the potato to the pan and set over a low heat to dry off the excess water, then mash with the oil.

Place the reserved cooking water in a jug and, while still warm (but not hot), add the yeast and stir to dissolve. Leave in a warm place for about 10 minutes until bubbles appear on the surface.

Stir the yeast mixture into the potato, then gradually stir in the remaining ingredients to form a dough. Tip the dough out on to a lightly floured surface and knead for 5 minutes until smooth, then place in a lightly oiled bowl, cover with oiled clingfilm and leave to rise in a warm place for 45 minutes–1 hour.

Knock back the dough and then divide into 8 pieces. Shape into balls, then flatten slightly. Transfer to a lightly oiled baking sheet and cover loosely with oiled clingfilm. Leave to prove for 30 minutes.

Bake in a preheated oven 220°C (425°F), Gas Mark 7, for 15–20 minutes until risen and golden brown and hollow when tapped on the base. Transfer to a wire rack and leave to cool for 5 minutes before serving.

For sweet potato & rosemary loaf, prepare the dough as above, using 2 tablespoons chopped rosemary in place of the onion seeds. Leave to rise as above for 45 minutes–1 hour, then knock back the dough and shape into a large round loaf. Score the top with a serrated knife, place on a lightly oiled baking sheet and bake as above for about 35 minutes.

shallot tarte tatin

Serves **4**

Preparation time **20 minutes**, plus cooling

Cooking time **40–45 minutes**

500 g (1 lb) **shallots**, peeled but left whole

50 g (2 oz) **butter**

2 tablespoons **light muscovado sugar**

3 tablespoons **cider vinegar**

a few **thyme sprigs**

250 g (8 oz) **ready-made puff pastry**, defrosted if frozen

salt and **black pepper**

Cut any large shallots in half. Melt the butter in a heatproof 20 cm (8 inch) frying pan, add the shallots and cook over a medium heat for 5 minutes until just beginning to colour. Add the sugar and cook for a further 5 minutes or until the shallots are caramelized, turning occasionally so that they cook evenly.

Stir in the vinegar, the leaves from the thyme sprigs and salt and pepper to taste and cook for 2 minutes.

Leave the shallots to cool for 20 minutes in the pan if it has a heatproof handle; if not, transfer to a heavy-based 20 cm (8 inch) round greased cake tin.

Roll out the pastry on a lightly floured surface and trim to a 20 cm (8 inch) circle. Arrange on top of the onions and tuck down the sides of the frying pan or cake tin.

Bake in a preheated oven, 200°C (400°F), Gas Mark 6, for 25–30 minutes until the pastry is well risen and golden. Leave to stand for 5 minutes, then loosen the edges with a knife. Cover with a serving plate or chopping board, invert the pan or cake tin on to the plate and then remove. Serve warm, cut into wedges, with a green leaf salad.

For shallot, apple & walnut tarte Tatin, follow the recipe above, reducing the shallots to 375 g (12 oz) and adding 1 dessert apple, cored, peeled and cut into 8 slices. Continue as above, adding 2 tablespoons walnut pieces with the sugar.

spiced flatbreads

Makes **4**
Preparation time **15 minutes**
Cooking time **6 minutes**

2 teaspoons **cumin seeds**
1 teaspoon **coriander seeds**
450 g (14½ oz) **strong
  white flour**
7 g (¼ oz) sachet **fast-action
  dried yeast**
1 teaspoon **caster sugar**
1 teaspoon **sea salt**
1 tablespoon **olive oil**
275 ml (9 fl oz) **warm water**

Toast the cumin and coriander seeds in a dry frying pan over a medium heat until aromatic, then crush with a pestle and mortar.

Mix together the flour, yeast, sugar, salt and toasted spices in a large bowl. Make a well in the centre, add the oil to the well and gradually stir into the flour with enough of the measurement water to form a moist, pliable dough.

Tip the dough out on to a lightly floured surface and knead for 5 minutes until smooth and elastic. Divide into 4 balls and roll out thinly on a lightly floured surface into long oval or round shapes. Prick all over with a fork and arrange on nonstick baking sheets.

Bake in a preheated oven, 220°C (425°F), Gas Mark 7, for 3 minutes. Turn over and bake for a further 3 minutes until golden brown. Serve immediately or wrap in a tea towel or foil to keep warm before serving.

For Eastern spiced garlic flatbreads, prepare the dough as above, omitting the cumin and coriander seeds and stirring in 2 teaspoons baharat or zahtar spice mix and 2 crushed garlic cloves. Shape and bake as above.

margherita scone-based pizza

Serves **4**
Preparation time **10 minutes**,
 plus cooling
Cooking time **20 minutes**

Tomato sauce
200 ml (7 fl oz) **passata**
 (sieved tomatoes)
2 tablespoons **tomato purée**
½ teaspoon **granulated sugar**
1 teaspoon **dried mixed
 herbs**

Pizza base
225 g (7½ oz) **self-
 raising flour**
1 teaspoon **salt**
50 g (2 oz) **butter**, diced
150 ml (¼ pint) **milk**

Topping
25 g (1 oz) **Cheddar
 cheese**, grated
245 g (8 oz) pack **mozzarella
 cheese**, drained and sliced
2 **tomatoes**, sliced
2 tablespoons fresh **pesto
 sauce** (see page 134 for
 homemade)
basil leaves, to garnish

Place all the ingredients for the sauce in a small saucepan and simmer over a low heat, stirring occasionally, for 5 minutes. Leave to cool.

Meanwhile, make the base. Place the flour and salt in a large bowl, then rub in the butter with your fingertips. Slowly pour in the milk and mix to form a soft dough.

Roll out the dough thinly on a large, lightly oiled baking sheet into a 30 cm (12 inch) round. Spread the tomato sauce over the pizza base and sprinkle with the Cheddar. Arrange the mozzarella and tomatoes over the top and drizzle over the pesto.

Bake in a preheated oven, 200°C (400°F), Gas Mark 6, for 15 minutes until the base is crisp and the cheese has melted. Serve hot with basil leaves scattered over.

For feta, spinach & black olive pizza, follow the recipe above to prepare the tomato sauce and pizza base. Place 150 g (5 oz) spinach leaves in a colander and pour over a kettle of boiling water to wilt the leaves, then refresh under cold running water, drain and squeeze out the excess water. Arrange over the pizza base and top with 150 g (5 oz) chopped feta cheese and 50 g (2 oz) pitted black olives. Bake as above.

blue cheese & thyme straws

Makes **40**
Preparation time **15 minutes**
Cooking time **15 minutes**

100 g (3½ oz) **plain flour**
2 teaspoons finely chopped
   thyme, plus extra
   for scattering
100 g (3½ oz) **unsalted
   butter**, chilled and diced
100 g (3½ oz) **firm blue
   cheese**, rind removed
   and grated
1 **egg yolk**
sea salt

Place the flour and thyme in a bowl or food processor. Add the butter and rub in with the fingertips or pulse until the mixture resembles breadcrumbs. Stir in the blue cheese and egg yolk and mix or process briefly to a dough.

Tip the dough out on to a lightly floured surface and lightly knead until smooth, then roll out into a rectangle 5 mm (¼ inch) thick. Cut into strips about 5 mm (¼ inch) wide and 9 cm (3½ inches) long.

Place slightly apart on a greased baking sheet. Sprinkle with sea salt and bake in a preheated oven, 200°C (400°F), Gas Mark 6, for about 15 minutes until golden.

Leave to cool slightly on the baking sheet, then transfer to a wire rack to cool completely. Serve scattered with extra thyme.

For olive twists, roll out 375 g (12 oz) ready-made puff pastry, defrosted if frozen, on a lightly floured surface into a 25 cm x 15 cm (10 inch x 6 inch) rectangle and cut in half. Beat 1 egg yolk with 1 tablespoon water, then brush thinly over one half. Spread thinly with 3 tablespoons black or green olive tapenade. Place the second piece on top and roll again to make a 24 cm (10 inch) square. Trim the edges and brush the surface with more of the egg yolk mixture. Cut the pastry in half, then cut each half across into 2 cm (about ¾ inch) strips. Twist each strip several times, then place on a lightly greased baking sheet. Sprinkle with sea salt and bake as above.

caper, cheese & polenta muffins

Makes **10**
Preparation time **10 minutes**
Cooking time **20–25 minutes**

175g (6 oz) **plain flour**
2 teaspoons **baking powder**
75 g (3 oz) **polenta** or
  cornmeal
2 tablespoons chopped **flat
  leaf parsley**
125 g (4 oz) **mature Cheddar
  cheese**, finely grated
2 tablespoons **capers**, drained
  and rinsed
1 teaspoon **salt**
1 teaspoon **ground black
  pepper**
1 large **egg**
75 g (3 oz) **butter**, melted
200 ml (7 fl oz) **milk**

Line a 12-hole muffin tin with 10 paper muffin cases.

Sift the flour and baking powder together into a large bowl. Add the polenta or cornmeal, parsley, three-quarters of the cheese, the capers, salt and pepper and mix well.

Beat the egg, melted butter and milk together in a separate bowl. Pour over the dry ingredients and stir until only just combined – the batter should be lumpy.

Spoon the mixture into the muffin cases so that they are about three-quarters full, then sprinkle the tops with the remaining cheese. Bake in a preheated oven, 190°C (375°F), Gas Mark 5, for 20–25 minutes until risen and firm.

Leave to cool in the tin for 5 minutes, then transfer to a wire rack to cool further. Serve warm.

For olive, goats' cheese & basil muffins, follow the above recipe to make the muffin mixture, omitting the parsley and capers, and using 125 g (4 oz) grated hard goats' cheese in place of the Cheddar. Stir in 100 g (3½ oz) chopped pitted black or green olives and 2 tablespoons chopped basil with the wet ingredients. Bake as above.

squash, sage & roquefort pie

Serves **6**
Preparation time **20 minutes**
Cooking time **35–40 minutes**

750g (1½ lb) peeled and
   deseeded **butternut
   squash**, cut into cubes
2 small **red onions**, quartered
1 tablespoon **olive oil**
50 g (2 oz) **butter**, melted
10 sheets of **filo pastry**,
   defrosted if frozen
small bunch of **sage**
250 g (9 oz) **ricotta cheese**,
   drained
100 g (3½ oz) **Roquefort
   cheese**
salt and **black pepper**

Spread the butternut squash and onions out in a roasting tin. Drizzle with the oil and season with pepper. Roast in a preheated oven, 190° C (375˚F), Gas Mark 5, for 15–20 minutes until just tender.

Meanwhile, brush a 28 cm (11 inch) round loose-bottomed flan tin with some of the melted butter. Lay a few sheets of filo pastry across it, slightly overlapping. Brush the overhanging filo with more butter. Continue layering the remaining filo, buttering as you go and slightly overlapping the sides of the tin.

Chop the sage roughly, reserving 6 leaves. Mix the ricotta and chopped sage together in a bowl and season well with salt and pepper, then spoon into the filo pastry case. Spoon over the roasted squash and onions, then crumble over the Roquefort and scatter over the reserved sage leaves.

Bake the pie in the oven for 20 minutes until golden. Serve warm with rocket leaves.

For Greek spinach, feta & pine nut pie, prepare the filo pastry case as above. Mix together 200 g (7 oz) each of drained ricotta cheese and crumbled feta cheese, 250 g (8 oz) baby spinach leaves, the juice of 1 lemon, 25 g (1 oz) pine nuts, 1 tablespoon raisins and 1 crushed garlic clove in a large bowl, and season well with salt and pepper. Spoon into the filo pastry case and bake as above.

banana & pecan loaf

Serves **8–10**
Preparation time **10 minutes**
Cooking time **50–60 minutes**

125 g (4 oz) **butter**, softened
225 g (8 oz) **soft light
brown sugar**
2 **eggs**
4 **ripe bananas**, mashed
100 ml (3½ fl oz) **buttermilk**
1 teaspoon **vanilla extract**
225 g (7½ oz) **plain flour**
1 teaspoon **bicarbonate
of soda**
1 teaspoon **baking powder**
½ teaspoon **salt**
125 g (4 oz) **pecan nuts**,
roughly chopped, plus
8 halves to decorate

Grease a 1 kg (2 lb) loaf tin. Beat the butter and sugar together in a large bowl with a hand-held electric whisk until pale and fluffy.

Whisk in the eggs, mashed bananas, buttermilk and vanilla extract until well combined.

Sift over the flour, bicarbonate of soda, baking powder and salt and gently fold in with a large metal spoon, then stir in the chopped pecan nuts.

Spoon the mixture into the prepared tin and arrange the pecan halves down the centre.

Bake in a preheated oven, 180°C (350°F), Gas Mark 4, for 50–60 minutes or until risen and golden brown and a skewer inserted into the centre comes out clean. Cover the top of the loaf with foil if it becomes too brown.

Leave the loaf to cool in the tin for a few minutes, then turn out on to a wire rack to cool completely before serving.

For banana, sultana & walnut bread, follow the recipe above, using 125 g (4 oz) chopped walnuts in place of the pecans and stirring in 125 g (4 oz) sultanas with the nuts. Arrange 8 walnut halves down the centre of the loaf and bake as above.

walnut & white chocolate cookies

Makes about **25**
Preparation time **15 minutes**
Cooking time **12–15 minutes**

1 **egg**
150 g (5 oz) **soft light
brown sugar**
2 tablespoons **caster sugar**
1 teaspoon **vanilla extract**
125 ml (4 fl oz) **vegetable oil**
65 g (2½ oz) **plain flour**
3 tablespoons **self-raising
flour**
¼ teaspoon **ground
cinnamon**
25 g (1 oz) **shredded coconut**
175 g (6 oz) **walnuts**, toasted
and chopped
125 g (4 oz) **white chocolate
chips**

Brush 2 baking sheets lightly with oil and line with
nonstick baking paper.

Beat the egg and sugars together in a bowl until pale
and creamy. Stir in the vanilla extract and oil. Sift in the
flours and cinnamon, then add the coconut, walnuts and
chocolate chips and mix well with a wooden spoon.

Shape rounded tablespoonfuls of the mixture into balls
and place on the prepared baking sheets, pressing the
mixture together with your fingertips if it is crumbly.
Bake in a preheated oven, 180°C (350°F), Gas Mark 4,
for 12–15 minutes or until golden.

Leave to cool for a few minutes on the sheets, then
transfer to a wire rack to cool completely.

For hazelnut & chocolate chip cookies, follow
the recipe above to make the cookie mixture, using
½ teaspoon ground ginger in place of the cinnamon,
toasted and chopped hazelnuts instead of the walnuts
and plain dark chocolate chips in place of the white.
Shape and bake as above.

196

tropical fruit cake

Serves **12**
Preparation time **15 minutes**,
  plus cooling
Cooking time **1 hour–
  1 hour 10 minutes**

100 g (3½ oz) **raisins**
250 g (8 oz) **mixed soft
  dried tropical fruit**, such as
  pineapple, mango, papaya
  and apricots, cut into
  small pieces
1 teaspoon **ground mixed
  spice**
1 teaspoon **ground ginger**
125 g (4 oz) **unsalted butter**,
  cut into cubes
125 g (4 oz) **soft light
  brown sugar**
150 ml (¼ pint) **cold water**
225 g (7½ oz) **self-raising
  flour**
1 **egg**, lightly beaten

Grease and line the base of a 1 kg (2 lb) loaf tin with nonstick baking paper (or use a loaf tin liner).

Place the raisins, dried tropical fruit, mixed spice, ginger, butter, sugar and measurement water in a saucepan. Warm over a low heat until the butter has melted, stirring occasionally with a wooden spoon, then bring to the boil.

Boil the fruit mixture for 5 minutes, then remove from the heat and leave to cool in the pan.

Stir the flour and beaten egg into the cooled fruit mixture until well combined, then spoon into the prepared tin.

Bake in the centre of a preheated oven, 150°C (300°F), Gas Mark 2, for 50–60 minutes or until a skewer inserted into the centre comes out clean.

Leave the cake to cool in the tin, then cut into slices to serve.

For traditional fruit cake, follow the recipe above to make the cake mixture, using a mixture of currants, chopped soft dried pitted dates, sultanas and glacé cherries in place of the dried tropical fruit and omitting the ground ginger. Bake as above.

apricot & cheese soda bread

Serves **8**
Preparation time **10 minutes**,
  plus cooling
Cooking time **35–40 minutes**

2 teaspoons **sunflower oil**
6 **spring onions**, thinly sliced
250 g (8 oz) **plain flour**
250 g (8 oz) **plain
  wholemeal flour**
2 teaspoons **bicarbonate
  of soda**
1 teaspoon **salt**
125 g (4 oz) **Wensleydale
  cheese with apricots**,
  crumbled
400 ml (14 fl oz) **buttermilk**,
  plus 2 tablespoons for
  brushing

Heat the oil in a small frying pan, add the spring onions and cook gently for 2 minutes until softened. Leave to cool slightly.

Sift the flours, bicarbonate of soda and salt into a large bowl. Stir in the cheese and spring onions. Make a well in the centre, add the buttermilk to the well and gradually stir into the flour. Bring the mixture together with your hands to form a soft, slightly sticky dough.

Tip the dough out on to a lightly floured surface and lightly knead for 1 minute, then shape into a ball.

Place on a lightly floured nonstick baking sheet and flatten slightly. Make a deep cross in the top with a serrated knife. Brush the top with the remaining buttermilk.

Bake in a preheated oven, 200°C (400°F), Gas Mark 6, for 30–35 minutes until the loaf sounds hollow when tapped on the base. Leave to cool on a wire rack. It is best served warm.

For apple & cheese soda bread, follow the recipe above to make the dough, adding 2 peeled, cored and chopped dessert apples and using 125 g (4 oz) grated mature Cheddar cheese in place of the Wensleydale cheese with apricots. Bake as above.

giant choc chip-orange cookies

Makes **12**
Preparation time **20 minutes**,
  plus chilling
Cooking time **10–12 minutes**

125 g (4 oz) **soft light brown
  sugar**
125 g (4 oz) **granulated
  sugar**
150 g (5 oz) **butter**, softened
2 teaspoons finely grated
  orange rind
1 large **egg**, lightly beaten
1 teaspoon **vanilla extract**
250 g (8 oz) **plain flour**
1 teaspoon **baking powder**
150 g (5 oz) good-quality
  **plain dark chocolate with
  orange**, roughly chopped
  into chunks

Beat the sugars, butter and orange rind together in a large bowl with a hand-held electric whisk until smooth and pale. Add the beaten egg and vanilla extract and beat until combined.

Sift in the flour and baking powder and mix with a wooden spoon until all the ingredients are combined. Stir in the chocolate chunks and bring the mixture together with your hands to form a dough.

Transfer the cookie dough to a large sheet of clingfilm, roll the dough into a wide 7 cm (3 inch) sausage shape and wrap in the clingfilm, twisting the ends to seal. Chill in the refrigerator for 30 minutes.

Slice the dough into about 12 x 1.5 cm (¾ inch) thick discs and place, spaced apart, on 2 large nonstick baking sheets. Bake in a preheated oven, 180°C (350°F), Gas Mark 4, for 10–12 minutes or until golden brown around the edge and slightly paler in the centre.

Leave on the baking sheets for 2 minutes, then transfer to a wire rack to cool completely.

For white chocolate & macadamia nut cookies,
prepare the cookie dough as above, omitting the orange rind and using 100 g (3½ oz) roughly chopped good-quality white chocolate in place of the plain dark chocolate and adding 50 g (2 oz) chopped macadamia nuts. Shape and bake as above.

lime & coconut drizzle cake

Serves **8**
Preparation time **20 minutes**
Cooking time **35–40 minutes**

200 g (7 oz) **unsalted butter**,
  softened
200 g (7 oz) **caster sugar**
finely grated rind and juice
  of 2 **limes**
3 **eggs**, lightly beaten
200 g (7 oz) **self-raising
  flour**, sifted
50 g (2 oz) **desiccated
  coconut**

Topping
4 tablespoons **caster sugar**
2 tablespoons **desiccated** or
  shredded coconut
finely pared long strands of
  lime rind

Grease a 20 cm (8 inch) round springform cake tin
and line the base with nonstick baking paper.

Beat the butter, sugar and grated lime rind together
in a large bowl with a hand-held electric whisk until
pale and fluffy. Beat in the eggs a little at a time,
adding 1 tablespoon of the flour if the mixture starts
to curdle, then fold in the flour and coconut with a
large metal spoon.

Spoon into the prepared tin and bake in the centre
of a preheated oven, 180°C (350 °F), Gas Mark 4, for
35–40 minutes until risen and golden and shrinking
away from the tin.

Leave to cool in the tin. While still warm, mix the sugar
for the topping with the lime juice and spoon over the
cake. Sprinkle over the coconut and lime rind strands.
Leave to cool completely.

For lime & coconut cupcakes, line a 12-hole
bun tin with paper cake cases. Beat together 125 g
(4 oz) each of softened butter and caster sugar and
the finely grated rind of 2 limes in a large bowl with a
hand-held electric whisk until pale and fluffy. Beat in
2 eggs and the juice of the limes. Fold in 150 g (5 oz)
self-raising flour, 1 teaspoon baking powder and 50 g
(2 oz) desiccated coconut. Divide between the cases.
Bake in a preheated oven, 180°C (350°F), Gas Mark
4, for 15–20 minutes until risen and golden. Leave to
cool on a wire rack. Mix the grated rind and juice of
1 lime with 175 g (6 oz) icing sugar and a few drops of
green colouring. Spoon over the cakes and sprinkle with
desiccated coconut.

desserts

plum & frangipane tart

Serves **8**
Preparation time **25 minutes**
Cooking time **45–50 minutes**

250 g (8 oz) **ready-made shortcrust pastry**, defrosted if frozen
6 tablespoons **plum conserve** or **jam**
150 g (5 oz) **unsalted butter**, softened
150 g (5 oz) **caster sugar**
3 **eggs**, lightly beaten
200 g (7 oz) **ground almonds**
½ teaspoon **almond extract**
100 g (3½ oz) **plain flour**
6 ripe **plums**, halved and stoned
25 g (1 oz) **flaked almonds**

Roll out the pastry on a lightly floured surface and use to line a 23 cm (9 inch) loose-bottomed flan tin. Spread half the plum conserve or jam over the base.

Beat the butter and sugar together in a large bowl with a hand-held electric whisk until pale and fluffy. Gradually beat in the eggs, then stir in the ground almonds, almond extract and flour. Spoon over the jam in the pastry case.

Arrange the plums, skin-side up, in circles over the almond mixture, starting from the outside, until it is covered. Sprinkle over the flaked almonds.

Place on a preheated baking sheet and bake in a preheated oven, 200°C (400°F), Gas Mark 6, for 40–45 minutes until risen and set.

Warm the remaining conserve or jam in a small saucepan, then brush over the top of the tart while the tart is still warm. Serve the tart warm in slices with a spoonful of double cream.

For apricot & almond tart, follow the recipe above to make the tart, using apricot conserve in place of the plum conserve or jam and 8–10 halved and stoned ripe apricots. Bake as above, then brush the top of the tart with the remaining warmed apricot conserve and serve in slices.

quick tiramisu

Serves **4–6**
Preparation time **15 minutes**,
   plus chilling

5 tablespoons strong
   espresso coffee
75 g (3 oz) **dark muscovado
   sugar**
4 tablespoons **coffee liqueur**
   or 3 tablespoons **brandy**
75 g (3 oz) **sponge finger
   biscuits**, broken into
   large pieces
400 g (13 oz) good-quality
   ready-made custard
250 g (8 oz) **mascarpone
   cheese**
1 teaspoon **vanilla extract**
75 g (3 oz) **plain dark
   chocolate**, finely chopped
sifted **cocoa powder,**
   for dusting

Mix the coffee with 2 tablespoons of the sugar and
the liqueur or brandy in a bowl. Toss the biscuits in the
mixture and turn into a serving dish, spooning over any
excess liquid.

Beat the custard, mascarpone and vanilla extract
together in a large bowl and spoon a third of the mixture
over the biscuits. Sprinkle with the remaining sugar,
then spoon over half the remaining custard. Scatter
with half the chopped chocolate, then spread with the
remaining custard and sprinkle with the remaining
chopped chocolate.

Chill for about 1 hour until set. Dust with sifted cocoa
powder and serve.

For raspberry tiramisu, place 125 g (4 oz) raspberries
in a saucepan with 1 tablespoon caster sugar and
2 tablespoons water. Bring to the boil, then remove from
the heat and beat with a wooden spoon to crush. Spoon
into a sieve set over a bowl and press through the sieve
to make a simple coulis. Prepare the other ingredients
as above, omitting the coffee liqueur, and use the coulis
to top the sponge finger biscuits before layering with
the mascarpone and custard mixture. Add a layer of
raspberries on top of the mascarpone. Dust with sifted
cocoa powder to serve.

pear & choc self-saucing pudding

Serves **6**

Preparation time **15 minutes**

Cooking time **40–45 minutes**

4 ripe **pears**, peeled, cored
and sliced

125 g (4 oz) **plain flour**

25 g (1 oz) **cocoa powder**

2 teaspoons **baking powder**

150 g (5 oz) **caster sugar**

200 ml (7 fl oz) **milk**

75 g (3 oz) **butter**, melted

1 **egg**, lightly beaten

Chocolate sauce

250 ml (8 fl oz) **water**

200 g (7 oz) **light brown
muscovado sugar**

1 tablespoon **cocoa powder**,
sifted

1 teaspoon **vanilla extract**

Arrange the pear slices in the bottom of a greased 1.5 litre (2½ pint) ovenproof dish.

Sift the flour, cocoa powder and baking powder together into a large bowl and add the caster sugar, milk, melted butter and egg. Beat with a hand-held electric whisk until smooth and creamy, then pour over the pears.

Combine all the sauce ingredients in a saucepan and heat over a low heat, stirring, until the sugar has dissolved. Bring to the boil, then pour over the pudding.

Bake in a preheated oven, 180°C (350°F), Gas Mark 4, for 35–40 minutes until the sponge is risen. Leave to stand for 3–4 minutes before serving. Serve with custard or vanilla ice cream.

For pear & caramel self-saucing pudding, prepare the sponge mixture as above, omitting the cocoa powder and reducing the caster sugar to 125 g (4 oz). Pour over the pears. For the caramel sauce, place 150 g (5 oz) light brown muscovado sugar in a saucepan with 4 tablespoons golden syrup and 250 ml (8 fl oz) water and heat over a low heat, stirring, until the sugar has dissolved. Bring to the boil, then pour over the pudding. Bake as above until risen and golden. Leave to stand for 5 minutes before serving.

pistachio chocolate brownies

Serves **6**
Preparation time **20 minutes**,
  plus cooling
Cooking time **30 minutes**

200 g (7 oz) **plain dark
  chocolate**, broken
  into pieces
200 g (7 oz) **butter**, diced
200 g (7 oz) **light
  muscovado sugar**
3 **eggs**
50 g (2 oz) **plain flour**
1 teaspoon **baking powder**
50 g (2 oz) **pistachio nuts**,
  roughly chopped
vanilla ice cream, to serve

Sauce
100 g (3½ oz) **plain dark
  chocolate**, broken
  into pieces
150 ml (¼ pint) **semi-
  skimmed milk**
2 tablespoons **light
  muscovado sugar**

Line a 20 cm (8 inch) square cake tin with nonstick baking paper.

Melt the chocolate and butter together in a heatproof bowl set over a saucepan of gently simmering water, stirring occasionally, making sure that the water doesn't touch the base of the bowl.

Whisk the sugar and eggs together in a large bowl with a hand-held electric whisk until pale, very thick and the whisk leaves a trail when lifted out of the mixture. Fold in the melted chocolate mixture, then the flour and baking powder.

Pour the mixture into the prepared tin and sprinkle with the pistachios. Bake in a preheated oven, 180°C (350°F), Gas Mark 4, for about 25 minutes until the top is crusty but the centre is still slightly soft. Leave to cool and harden in the tin.

Make the sauce. Heat all the sauce ingredients together gently in a saucepan, stirring until smooth.

Lift the brownies out of the tin using the paper. Cut into small squares, lift off the paper and transfer to serving plates. Add scoops of vanilla ice cream and serve with the warm chocolate sauce.

For white chocolate & cranberry blondies, melt 200 g (7 oz) white chocolate, broken into pieces, with 125 g (4 oz) diced butter as above. Whisk 150 g (5 oz) caster sugar with 3 eggs as above, then fold in the melted chocolate mixture. Fold in 150 g (5 oz) self-raising flour and 50 g (2 oz) dried cranberries. Bake as above.

chocolate & chilli mousse cake

Serves **8–10**
Preparation time **20 minutes**,
   plus cooling and chilling
Cooking time **35 minutes**

300 g (10 oz) good-quality
   **plain dark chocolate with
   chilli** (70% cocoa solids),
   broken into pieces
150 g (5 oz) **unsalted butter**,
   diced
6 **eggs**, separated
125 g (4 oz) **caster sugar**

Chilli syrup
1 **red chilli**, thinly sliced
grated rind and juice of 1 **lime**
100 g (3½ oz) **golden caster
   sugar**
150 ml (¼ pint) **water**

Line the base of a 20 cm (8 inch) springform cake
tin with nonstick baking paper. Melt the chocolate and
butter in a heatproof bowl set over a saucepan of gently
simmering water, stirring occasionally, making sure the
water doesn't touch the base of the bowl. Meanwhile,
whisk the egg yolks with the sugar in a bowl with a
hand-held electric whisk until pale and thick. Stir in the
melted chocolate mix.

Whisk the egg whites in a separate large, grease-
free bowl until they form soft peaks. Fold a couple of
tablespoons of the egg white into the chocolate mixture
to loosen, then fold in the remaining egg white with a
metal spoon. Pour the mixture into the prepared tin and
bake in a preheated oven, 180°C (350°F), Gas Mark 4,
for 20 minutes. Remove from the oven, cover with foil
(to prevent a crust forming) and leave to cool. Chill in
the refrigerator for at least 4 hours or overnight.

Make the syrup. Combine all the syrup ingredients in a
small saucepan and heat over a low heat, stirring, until
the sugar has dissolved. Bring to the boil, then simmer
for 10 minutes until syrupy. Leave to cool. Remove the
cake from the refrigerator 30 minutes before serving in
slices, with the syrup poured over.

For chocolate, whisky & ginger mousse cake,
prepare the cake mix as above, using 300 g (10 oz)
plain dark chocolate with ginger, broken into pieces,
in place of the plain dark chocolate with chilli and
adding 2 tablespoons whisky. Bake, cool and chill as
above. Whisk 300 ml (½ pint) whipping cream with
1 tablespoon whisky and spoon over the cake. Dust
with cocoa powder and serve.

melon, ginger & lime sorbet

Serves **4**
Preparation time **15 minutes**,
plus freezing

1 large ripe **Charentais** or
Galia melon, chilled
150 g (5 oz) **caster sugar**
1 tablespoon peeled and finely
grated **fresh root ginger**
juice of 2 **limes**

Cut the melon in half and remove and discard the seeds, then roughly chop the flesh – you need about 450 g (14½ oz). Place in a food processor with the sugar, ginger and lime juice, then blend until smooth.

Transfer the sorbet to an ice cream maker and process according to the manufacturer's instructions. If you don't have an ice cream maker, place the mixture in a freezer-proof container and freeze for about 2–3 hours or until ice crystals have appeared on the surface. Beat with a hand-held electric whisk until smooth, then return to the freezer. Repeat this process twice more until you have a fine-textured sorbet and freeze until firm.

Remove the sorbet from the freezer 10 minutes before serving. Serve, scooped into glasses with a wafer.

For honeydew melon granita, place 75 g (3 oz) caster sugar in a saucepan with 150 ml (¼ pint) water and stir over a low heat until dissolved, then bring to the boil. Remove from the heat and leave to cool, then place in a food processor with 450 g (14½ oz) chopped Honeydew melon flesh and 2 tablespoons melon liqueur (optional) and blend until smooth. Transfer to a shallow freezer-proof container and freeze for 1 hour or until ice crystals appear at the edges. Stir the ice into the centre and return to the freezer. Stir and refreeze a few more times until frozen all over. To serve, scrape the granita with a fork and serve immediately.

coffee latte custards

Serves **6**

Preparation time **20 minutes**,
  plus cooling and chilling

Cooking time **30 minutes**

2 **eggs**

2 **egg yolks**

397 g (13¾ oz) can **full-fat
  condensed milk**

200 ml (7 fl oz) **strong black
  coffee**, cooled

150 ml (¼ pint) **double cream**

sifted **cocoa powder**,
  for dusting

chocolate wafer sticks,
  to serve

Whisk the eggs, egg yolks and condensed milk together in a bowl until just mixed. Gradually whisk in the coffee until blended.

Strain the mixture, then pour into 6 x 125 ml (4 fl oz) greased coffee cups. Transfer the cups to a roasting tin. Pour hot water into the tin to come halfway up the sides of the cups, then bake in a preheated oven, 160°C (325°F), Gas Mark 3, for 30 minutes until just set.

Lift the cups out of the water and leave the custards to cool, then transfer to the refrigerator and chill for 4–5 hours.

Whip the cream in a bowl until it forms soft swirls. Spoon the cream over the top of the custards, dust with a little sifted cocoa powder and serve with chocolate wafer sticks.

For dark chocolate custards, bring 450 ml (¾ pint) milk and 150 ml (¼ pint) double cream just to the boil in a saucepan. Add 200 g (7 oz) plain dark chocolate, broken into pieces, and leave to melt. Mix 2 eggs and 2 egg yolks with 50 g (2 oz) caster sugar and ¼ teaspoon ground cinnamon, then gradually mix in the chocolate mixture and stir until smooth. Strain into small dishes and bake as above. After cooling and chilling, top with whipped cream and chocolate curls.

caramel & honeycomb mousse

Serves **6**
Preparation time **15 minutes**,
  plus cooling and chilling

150 g (5 oz) good-quality
  milk chocolate, broken
  into pieces
200 g (7 oz) canned **caramel**
250 ml (8 fl oz) **double cream**
40 g (1½ oz) **bar milk
  chocolate with golden
  honeycomb**, roughly
  chopped, plus extra
  to decorate

Melt the chocolate in a heatproof bowl set over a saucepan of gently simmering water, stirring occasionally, making sure that the water doesn't touch the base of the bowl. Leave to cool slightly.

Place the caramel in a bowl with the cream and whisk with a hand-held electric whisk until the mixture starts to thicken and leaves a trail.

Stir a little of the caramel mixture into the melted chocolate, then fold the chocolate mixture into the caramel mixture until well combined. Stir in the chocolate honeycomb.

Spoon into 6 small glasses and chill for 15–30 minutes (no longer, otherwise the honeycomb will start to dissolve). Decorate with a little extra chocolate honeycomb before serving.

For homemade honeycomb, heat 5 tablespoons granulated sugar and 2 tablespoons golden syrup in a heavy-based saucepan over a medium heat until the sugar melts, then boil the mixture until it turns a deep, golden caramel. Whisk in 1 teaspoon bicarbonate of soda (this will make it foam up), then quickly pour on to an oiled baking sheet set on a chopping board. Leave to cool completely, then break into small pieces. Serve as a topping for ice cream.

classic lemon tart

Serves **8**
Preparation time **20 minutes**,
   plus chilling and cooling
Cooking time **45–50 minutes**

450 g (14½ oz) **ready-made
   sweet shortcrust pastry**,
   defrosted if frozen
3 **eggs**
1 **egg yolk**
450 ml (¾ pint) **double cream**
100 g (3½ oz) **caster sugar**
150 ml (¼ pint) freshly
   squeezed **lemon juice**
sifted **icing sugar**, for dusting

Roll out the pastry thinly on a lightly floured surface and use it to line a 25 cm (10 inch) fluted flan tin. Prick the pastry case with a fork and then chill in the refrigerator for 15 minutes.

Line the pastry case with nonstick baking paper, fill with dried macaroni or beans and bake in a preheated oven, 190°C (375°F), Gas Mark 5, for 15 minutes. Remove the paper and macaroni or beans and bake for a further 10 minutes until crisp and golden. Remove from the oven and reduce the temperature to 150°C (300°F), Gas Mark 2.

Beat the eggs, egg yolk, cream, caster sugar and lemon juice together in a bowl, then pour into the pastry case.

Bake for 20–25 minutes until the filling is just set. Leave the tart to cool in the tin, then dust with sifted icing sugar and serve.

For mixed berries with cassis, to serve as an accompaniment, halve or slice 250 g (8 oz) fresh strawberries, depending on their size, and mix with 125 g (4 oz) each of fresh raspberries and blueberries, 3 tablespoons caster sugar and 2 tablespoons crème de cassis. Leave to soak for 1 hour before serving with the tart.

moroccan rice pudding

Serves 4
Preparation time **5 minutes**
Cooking time **30 minutes**

100 g (3½ oz) **pudding rice**,
  rinsed and drained
50 g (2 oz) **caster sugar**
2 **cinnamon sticks**
1 teaspoon **vanilla bean**
  paste
450 ml (¾ pint) **water**
400 g (13 oz) can **evaporated**
  milk
2 teaspoons **rosewater**
50 g (2 oz) **pistachio nuts**,
  roughly chopped
a few **edible rose petals**
  (optional)

Place the rice, sugar, cinnamon sticks, vanilla bean paste and measurement water in a saucepan and bring to the boil.

Reduce the heat and simmer the rice, uncovered, for 20 minutes. Stir in the evaporated milk and rosewater and simmer for a further 10 minutes until the rice is tender. Remove the cinnamon sticks.

Pour the rice pudding into warmed serving dishes and sprinkle with the pistachios and rose petals, if liked. Serve immediately.

For orange & cardamom rice pudding, place the rinsed and drained pudding rice, the caster sugar, measurement water, the grated rind and juice of 1 orange and 6 crushed cardamom pods in a saucepan. Bring to the boil, then reduce the heat and simmer for 25 minutes. Stir in the evaporated milk and cook for a further 5 minutes until the rice is tender. Serve decorated with toasted flaked almonds.

white choc & raspberry tiramisu

Serves **6**
Preparation time **20 minutes**

3 teaspoons **instant coffee**
7 tablespoons **icing sugar**
250 ml (8 fl oz) **boiling water**
12 **sponge finger biscuits**
   (about 100 g/3½ oz)
250 g (8 oz) **mascarpone
   cheese**
150 ml (¼ pint) **double cream**
3 tablespoons **kirsch**
   (optional)
250 g (8 oz) **fresh
   raspberries**
75 g (3 oz) **white chocolate**,
   diced

Place the coffee and 4 tablespoons of the sugar in a shallow dish, pour over the measurement water and stir until dissolved.

Dip 6 biscuits, one at a time, into the coffee mixture, then crumble into the bases of 6 glass tumblers.

Combine the mascarpone with the remaining sugar in a bowl, then gradually whisk in the cream until smooth. Stir in the kirsch, if using, then divide half the mixture between the glasses.

Crumble half the raspberries over the top of the mascarpone mixture in the glasses, then sprinkle with half the chocolate. Dip the remaining biscuits in the coffee mix, crumble and add to the glasses.

Add the remaining mascarpone mixture and whole raspberries to the glasses, finishing with a sprinkling of the remaining chocolate. Serve immediately or chill until required.

For classic tiramisu, mix the mascarpone with 3 tablespoons icing sugar and the cream as above, stirring in 3 tablespoons Kahlúa coffee liqueur or brandy in place of the kirsch. Prepare the coffee-dipped sponge finger biscuits as above, then layer in one large dish with the mascarpone mixture and 75 g (3 oz) diced plain dark chocolate, omitting the raspberries and white chocolate.

rhubarb & raspberry crumble

Serves **4**
Preparation time **10 minutes**
Cooking time **25 minutes**

500 g (1 lb) fresh or defrosted
  frozen **rhubarb**, sliced
125 g (4 oz) fresh or frozen
  raspberries
50 g (2 oz) **soft light
  brown sugar**
3 tablespoons **orange juice**
raspberry ripple ice cream,
  to serve

Crumble topping
200 g (7 oz) **plain flour**
pinch of **salt**
150 g (5 oz) **unsalted
  butter**, diced
50 g (2 oz) **soft light
  brown sugar**

Make the crumble topping. Combine the flour and salt in a bowl, add the butter and rub in with the fingertips until the mixture resembles breadcrumbs. Stir in the sugar.

Mix the fruits, the sugar and orange juice together in a separate bowl, then tip into a greased ovenproof dish. Sprinkle over the topping and bake in a preheated oven, 200°C (400°F), Gas Mark 6, for about 25 minutes or until golden brown and bubbling.

Serve the crumble hot with raspberry ripple ice cream.

For apple & blackberry crumble, follow the recipe above, using 450 g (14½ oz) each of apples, peeled and chopped, and fresh or frozen blackberries in place of the rhubarb and raspberries. Alternatively, you could use 450 g (14½ oz) plums, stoned and quartered, and 4 peeled, cored and thinly sliced ripe pears.

hazelnut meringue gateau

Serves **6–8**
Preparation time **20 minutes**,
  plus cooling
Cooking time **30 minutes**

4 **egg whites**
275 g (9 oz) **caster sugar**
½ teaspoon **white wine
  vinegar**
1 teaspoon **vanilla extract**
1 teaspoon **cornflour**
150 g (5 oz) **toasted
  hazelnuts**, ground
300 ml (½ pint) **double cream**
150 g (5 oz) **fresh
  raspberries**
25 g (1 oz) **plain dark
  chocolate**, melted

Brush 2 x 20 cm (8 inch) round cake tins lightly with oil
and line the bases with nonstick baking paper.

Whisk the egg whites in a large, grease-free bowl with
a hand-held electric whisk until they form stiff peaks.
Gradually whisk in the sugar until thick and glossy.
Gently fold in the vinegar, vanilla extract, cornflour
and hazelnuts.

Divide the mixture between the prepared tins and bake
in a preheated oven, 180°C (350°F), Gas Mark 4 for
30 minutes.

Leave to cool in the tins for 10 minutes, then turn out
carefully on to a wire rack and peel off the paper.

Whip the cream in a bowl until it forms soft peaks.
Spread over the base of 1 meringue and top with the
raspberries, then sandwich together with the remaining
meringue. Drizzle over the melted chocolate and chill
until ready to serve.

For chocolate & raspberry Eton mess, whip 300 ml
(½ pint) double cream with 2 tablespoons icing sugar
in a bowl until it forms soft peaks, then stir in 450 ml
(¾ pint) Greek yogurt. Gently stir in 300 g (10 oz)
fresh raspberries and 8 crushed meringue nests. Ripple
through with 6 tablespoons ready-made chocolate
sauce and divide between 6–8 glasses. Chill until ready
to serve.

fig & honey pots

Serves **4**
Preparation time **10 minutes**,
  plus chilling

6 **ripe fresh figs**, thinly sliced,
  plus 2 extra, cut into wedges,
  to decorate (optional)
450 ml (¾ pint) **Greek yogurt**
4 tablespoons **clear honey**
2 tablespoons chopped
  pistachio nuts

Arrange the fig slices snugly in the bottom of 4 glasses or glass bowls. Spoon the yogurt over the figs and chill in the refrigerator for 10–15 minutes.

Drizzle 1 tablespoon honey over each dessert and sprinkle the pistachio nuts on top. Decorate with the wedges of fig, if liked, before serving.

For hot figs with honey, heat a griddle pan or large frying pan over a medium-high heat, and when hot, add 8 whole ripe fresh figs and cook for 8 minutes, turning occasionally, until charred on the outside. Alternatively, cook under a preheated grill. Remove and cut in half. Divide between serving plates, top each with 1 tablespoonful of Greek yogurt and drizzle with a little clear honey.

index

acknowledgements

Executive editor: Eleanor Maxfield
Designer: Eoghan O'Brien
Editor: Jo Wilson
Copy-editor: Jo Richardson
Art direction and design: Penny Stock
Photographer: William Shaw
Home economy: Denise Smart
Stylist: Liz Hippisley
Production controller: Sarah Kramer

Photography copyright © Octopus Publishing Group
Limited/William Shaw, except the following: copyright
© Octopus Publishing Group 229; Frank Adam 71;
Stephen Conroy 77, 81, 85, 89, 115, 119, 197, 231;
Will Heap 10, 12, 15, 149, 211, 221; William Lingwood
27, 93; David Loftus 123; Neil Mersh 235; Lis Parsons
101, 111, 225; William Reavell 8, 9; Gareth Sambidge
41; William Shaw 107, 127, 183, 189, 215; Ian Wallace
97, 179.